W9-BMD-629

RAISE THE ROOF

RAISE THE ROOF
Appliquéd Houses and Buildings

Tonee White

Martingale®
& COMPANY

Raise the Roof: Appliquéd Houses and Buildings
© 2005 by Tonee White

That Patchwork Place® is an imprint of
Martingale & Company®.

Martingale & Company
20205 144th Avenue NE
Woodinville, WA 98072-8478 USA
www.martingale-pub.com

No part of this product may be reproduced in
any form, unless otherwise stated, in which case
reproduction is limited to the use of the purchaser.
The written instructions, photographs, designs,
projects, and patterns are intended for the personal,
noncommercial use of the retail purchaser and are
under federal copyright laws; they are not to be
reproduced by any electronic, mechanical, or other
means, including informational storage or retrieval
systems, for commercial use. Permission is granted to
photocopy patterns for the personal use of the retail
purchaser.

The information in this book is presented in
good faith, but no warranty is given nor results
guaranteed. Since Martingale & Company has no
control over choice of materials or procedures, the
company assumes no responsibility for the use of
this information.

Printed in China
10 09 08 07 06 05   8 7 6 5 4 3 2 1

Library of Congress Cataloging-in-Publication Data
White, Tonee.
    Raise the roof : appliquéd houses and
    buildings / Tonee White.
        p. cm.
    ISBN 1-56477-609-3
    1. Appliqué—Patterns. 2. Quilting.
    3. Buildings in art. 4. Dwellings in art. I. Title.
    TT779.W556 2005
    746.44'5041—dc22
                                            2005003889

Credits

President • Nancy J. Martin
CEO • Daniel J. Martin
VP and General Manager • Tom Wierzbicki
Publisher • Jane Hamada
Editorial Director • Mary V. Green
Managing Editor • Tina Cook
Technical Editor • Karen Costello Soltys
Copy Editor • Liz McGehee
Design Director • Stan Green
Illustrator • Laurel Strand
Cover and Text Designer • Shelly Garrison
Photographer • Brent Kane

Mission Statement
Dedicated to providing quality products
and service to inspire creativity.

CONTENTS

PATTERN SHEETS

INTRODUCTION

I am so pleased to have the opportunity to share these quilts with you. I have designed and constructed these pieces over the last 10 years, and I must say, I honed my appliqué and piecing skills creating them. I have always loved house blocks of any type. The old houses came first. One or two brought farmhouses to mind, which led to barns. After that the lighthouses and churches were a natural progression. I continue to design buildings of all sorts—they are a favorite subject of mine.

These quilts are not particularly difficult to make, but they are not as quickly constructed as the quilts I had become accustomed to making using my Appliquilt technique. With that method, I appliqué onto the layered quilt and the appliqué stitches do double duty as quilting stitches. Most of the projects in this book, however, are

PINE RIDGE PONIES

appliquéd first; then the quilts are layered and quilted—some solely by machine, others with a mix of machine and hand stitches.

I feel blessed to have had a wonderful teacher who taught me needle-turn appliqué. Judy Maxwell was very nurturing, supportive, and positive when the other teachers I had in that first year were sticklers for precision and perfection. Because of her positive encouragement, my creativity could shine through and I began to design with the self-assurance that I could be successful, even though I was a novice.

I'm pleased you have chosen this book and my designs to make for yourself. A confident beginner will be successful and will only become more confident with the completion of one of these projects. Most of all—have fun.

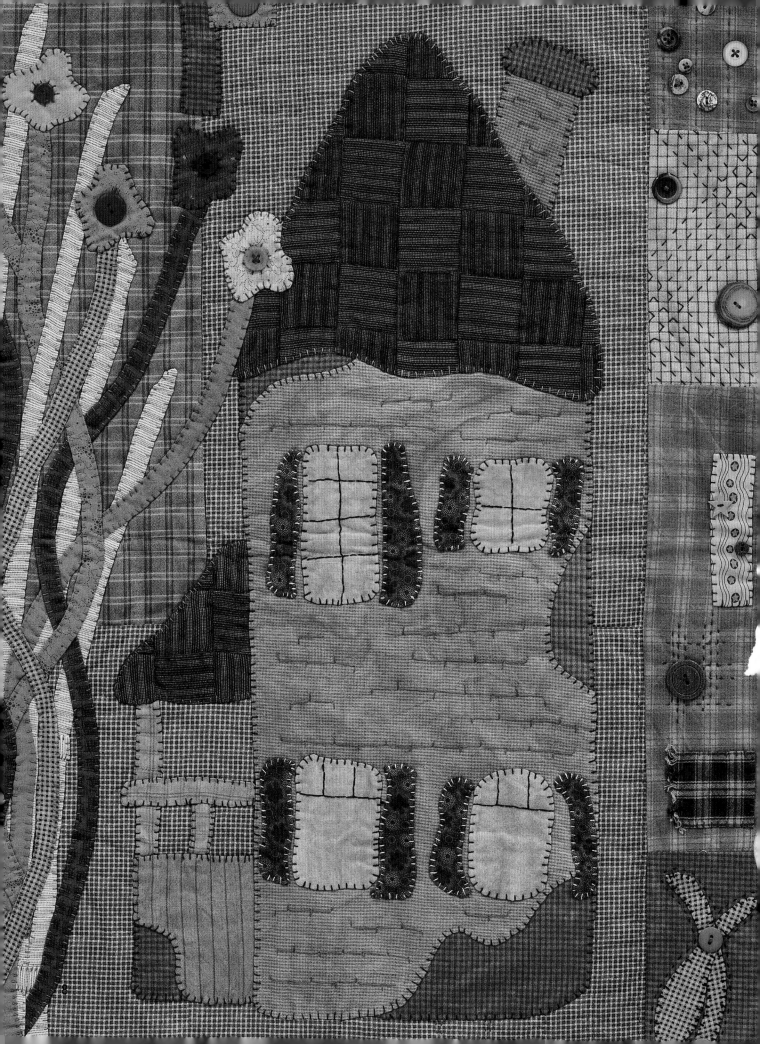

MATERIALS AND TOOLS

Most likely, you already have all the tools and supplies you need to make any of the quilts in this book. Let's just talk a little bit about fabric choices, because with my *Raise the Roof* quilts, fabric selection can go a long way toward making a successful finished quilt. Also, because I sometimes like to Appliquilt my projects, I'll cover the types of batting, threads, and needles I like to use for this style of quiltmaking.

Fabric

When I began to gather fabric for "Old Homesteads," which was the first project I made for this collection, there were very few fabrics available that mimicked the look of bricks, wood, stone, or other building materials. Today, that has all changed and we are so fortunate with the fabric selection in stores now. That said, you can make any of the projects in this book without using building-material fabrics. There is a wealth of incredible fabrics available in all colors and textures that would be perfect for the projects in this book.

Fabric selection is one of the many opportunities you have to express your creativity. Aside from using realistic-looking bricks and rock fabrics, you can use any number of other prints, plaids, and stripes to create the buildings you're seeing in your mind's eye. If you're having trouble finding brick fabric, think visual texture. If the stone fabrics you see aren't quite the right scale for your quilt, again think visual texture. Varied prints, plaids, and stripes in the same color, even if they aren't specific building-material prints, can give you enough contrast to define pieces of a wall or roof. Making any of the projects in this book will give you the opportunity to learn more about fabric selection and really hone your skills in this area. Don't be afraid to make a mistake. Those lessons learned are ones we always remember. And sometimes that oddball fabric is just what our quilts needed.

Because I do my fabric shopping almost entirely in quilt shops, I primarily use 100%-cotton fabrics. Having said that, you can get wonderful texture with wool, rayon, knits, lamés, and more. There are no rules when it comes to fabric. For fun, you may want to browse in shops that carry dressmaking fabrics, as well as little boutiques or antique shops, to find just the right textured fabric for your quilt. Why limit yourself?

Batting

I prefer cotton batting for all the quilts I make, with one exception—Pellon fleece. It is a very lightweight polyester batting; you can see through it. For as lightweight as it is, it holds its shape, and therefore a quilt layered with this batting has a better chance to hang straight.

The disadvantage with this product is that it is only 45" wide. If you piece the fleece, you defeat its advantage of holding its shape unless you piece it perfectly. I don't want the responsibility of having to achieve perfection, so I generally only use this batting for smaller wall hangings, such as "Tattersall Lane" on page 58.

Usually, I machine quilt my projects, so any brand of cotton batting seems to work well; hand needling isn't a concern for me. When Appliquilting motifs (hand appliquéing and quilting all in one step), any lightweight cotton or mostly cotton batting works well.

Needles and Thread

Needle preference can be as personal as your choice of coffee at the local Starbucks. The size and length of the shaft, the size and shape of the eye, as well as the task at hand are all to be considered. Appliquilting with size 8 pearl cotton requires a different-size needle than the traditional hand appliqué done on most of the quilts in this book.

For traditional appliqué, I prefer size 11 Sharps. These needles are slim with a small eye, but at the same time, they're quite sturdy. Straw needles are much longer than Sharps and bend more easily; I have even broken a few. I have never broken a Sharp.

When it comes to thread for traditional appliqué, I prefer 60-weight cotton embroidery thread. It is easier to thread than standard sewing thread in the size 11 needles I like, and it draws through fabric easily. I have used silk thread and like the way it seemingly disappears into the fabric. However, because it is so fine, it slips out of the needle easily and I have to rethread the needle often. Frankly, I'd rather be stitching than threading my needle.

For Appliquilting, I use size 7 embroidery needles. They are long enough to give me good control when stitching. Plus, I can thread them easily with pearl cotton, topstitching thread, or two to three strands of embroidery floss—the threads I use most often for Appliquilting. Another fun thread choice for Appliquilting is linen thread, which is a 40/2 weight and has the look of miniature jute. It draws through fabric easily and goes well with virtually anything.

CONSTRUCTION TECHNIQUES

Most of the projects in the book are hand appliquéd using the needle-turn method. Some have additional appliqués added after the quilting and binding are finished. For those, I appliqué through all layers of the quilt using my technique called Appliquilt or Appliquilting. You may already have a favorite method for appliqué, but if you'd like an explanation of how I make and use templates, make vines and other narrow pieces like fences and porch posts, and generally put my quilts together, browse through the following section for pointers.

Appliqué Templates

I make plastic templates for each appliqué motif. Plastic gives a firm edge for tracing, which in turn makes for accurate duplication. I like keeping a permanent record of my designs, and plastic templates retain their shape and are easy to store. I like to be able to go to previous designs and reuse motifs, such as stars, leaves, and flowers.

1. Trace the motif to the rougher-feeling side of the template plastic using a soft lead pencil or fine-point permanent marker. Cut out the template with paper or craft scissors.

2. Place the template on the right side of the fabric and trace around the entire template with a lead or chalk pencil. The main objective is to be able to see the traced line.

3. Using sharp scissors, cut out the fabric ¼" outside the traced line.

Cut out the shape,
leaving a ¼" seam allowance.

4. For some patterns, reverse appliqué is the easiest method to use. In this method, an interior shape is cut out of the top layer of fabric and the edges are appliquéd to a second fabric beneath it. For instance, the windows of the house blocks in "Home Sweet Home" on page 26 are reverse appliquéd. To make the template, trace the window rectangle onto the main house template. Then cut out the window shape from the plastic template and trace around this shape onto the house fabric. After cutting out the house itself from fabric, cut out the windows, cutting ¼" *inside* the drawn window lines. Clip the corners to the marked line. Then turn the window edges under on the marked line and appliqué them to the window fabric, which is placed in the opening between the background and the house.

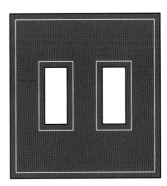

Cut ¼" inside the window lines.

5. Finally, for the very large patterns in this book, such as the irregularly shaped backgrounds for the lighthouses in "Beacons of Light" on page 16, freezer-paper templates may be easier to use. Trace the background shapes onto the dull (uncoated) side of the freezer paper. Cut out the template on the drawn line. Press the freezer paper, shiny surface down, to the right side of the fabric. Trace around the edge of the paper. Cut out the background shape, cutting ¼" outside the drawn line. Remove the freezer paper.

Vines, Fences, Railings, and Casings

I used a free-form method to make most of the vines, fences, railings, and window casings. By not carefully measuring and drawing lines for folding under seam allowances, I made the motifs look more natural. They were also easier to execute. You can make them perfectly straight if you like, but I prefer the more casual, folk-art look. I also generally cut the strips used for fences and vines freehand with a scissors, rather than more precisely with a ruler and rotary cutter. In the project directions, you'll see dimensions given for cutting strips for fences, vines, window casings, and such. Use these dimensions as a guideline for cutting by hand for a casual look; use them specifically if you'd like a more exact line.

When working with these strips, I do not mark a turn-under line, but rather I judge a ⅛" to ¼" seam allowance by eye. This allows me to change the width of a rail fence from narrow at one end to wider at the other, or to make a more natural-looking vine. By using a ⅛" seam allowance, I can also make a porch railing narrower than ¼", which I often like to do. Of course, if you prefer straight and even motifs, measure carefully and draw the motifs with a ruler.

Use thread to match the motif and use the traditional appliqué stitch described at right. Using contrasting threads and larger primitive stitches on small motifs, such as the fences on "Old Homesteads" and "Barn Raising," can be confusing to the eye; the line of the motif becomes obscured by the color and size of the stitches.

The Stitches

The quilts in this book use three types of hand stitching: traditional appliqué, needle-turn Appliquilting, and decorative embroidery. Following, you'll find a description of each of the methods I used to create the quilts.

Traditional Appliqué

The stitch used most often in the traditional appliqué is the blind hem stitch or "tack" stitch. Concealing the stitches is the desired effect, so the thread color should closely match the motif, and the stitches should be small and close together.

To start, bring the threaded needle up from under the motif, so that the needle pierces the fabric right on the line you marked when you traced around the template. Then, using the tip of your needle, fold the seam allowance under the motif along the drawn line and hold it in place with the thumb of your opposite hand. Take a stitch down into the background fabric with your needle right next to the fold where your needle came up from behind the motif. Bring your needle back up on the traced line ¹⁄₁₆" to ⅛" from the previous stitch.

Pull the thread through the fabric, but don't pull so tightly that it puckers the edge of your appliqué. Continue making stitches in this manner, catching just a few threads of the background fabric and then a few of the appliqué motif. When sewing straight areas, you can space the stitches ⅛" apart, but on curves, place the stitches closer together to create a smooth, pucker-free curve.

To end stitching, bring the needle to the wrong side of the work and take a few tiny backstitches, taking care not to sew through to the right side of the appliqué motif.

Needle-Turn Appliquilting

The overcast stitch I use in the needle-turn Appliquilt method resembles a blanket stitch but is easier and faster for me to do. You can use this stitch when Appliquilting through all layers of the quilt or to simply appliqué a motif to a background fabric. Generally, a heavier-weight thread is used, especially when stitching through all three quilt layers. Using a contrasting-color thread will give added impact to the finished stitches.

The difference between this stitch and the traditional appliqué stitch discussed above is *where* you bring your needle up through the motif. Traditionally, the thread comes up on the turn-under line, but when you use the overcast stitch, you bring the needle up ⅛" to ¼" inside the traced line and back down into the background fabric just outside the motif edge. As a result, the thread shows up on the motif, adding a decorative element to the appliqué.

To Appliquilt, assemble the three layers of background, batting, and backing and baste them together. Using the heavier thread and overcast stitch, appliqué the motifs by pushing your needle through not only the background block but also the batting and the backing on a diagonal (mostly through the batting) and coming up ⅛" to ¼" inside the seam allowance to begin your next stitch.

Overcast stitch

Embroidery

Some of the quilts in this book include architectural details that would be too small or tedious to try to appliqué, so they are added with simple embroidery stitches instead. Below are illustrations of the various stitches I used.

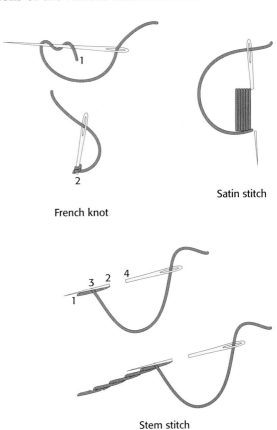

French knot

Satin stitch

Stem stitch

Finishing Your Quilt

Traditionally, layering the quilt top, batting, and backing, and then quilting the quilt are done after all patchwork and appliqué are completed. Some of the quilts in this book, however, utilize my Appliquilting technique, and therefore, these steps to finishing your quilt actually happen before some of the appliqués are added. Either way, if you need some guidance for the quilting and binding steps, read through the following sections.

Layering and Basting

1. With the right side down, press your entire quilt top well, making sure all seams are pressed as flat as possible.

2. Measure the quilt top carefully and cut the backing and batting 4" to 6" longer and wider so that you will have at least 2" extra all around your quilt top for insurance.

3. Spread the backing, right side down, on a hard surface, such as a large table or floor. Tape or clamp the backing to the table, tape it to the floor, or pin it to the carpet so that it is taut but not stretched. Lay the batting onto the center of the backing. Smooth it out with your hands to eliminate any wrinkles, lumps, or bumps. Cotton batting tends to adhere to cotton fabric, so smooth it carefully. Then lay your quilt top right side up on the center of your batting. Check to make sure it is aligned properly with your backing fabric. Smooth the top well as you did with the batting.

    Note: Quite often, quilt shops allow quilters to take advantage of their classroom tables for basting. You can push two tables together if necessary.

4. Pin baste if you plan to machine quilt, placing a safety pin every 4" to 6" in a grid across the entire surface of the quilt. Do not close the pins until they are all placed. Disturbing the three layers to close a pin, multiplied by the number of pins used, can lead to puckers or pleats in the layers.

    If you choose to hand quilt, I suggest you thread baste. Cut the thread two or three times the normal length for hand sewing, use a long darning needle, and take stitches that are 1" to 2" long. You can take a number of stitches at a time before drawing the thread through the layers. Sew in a 4" grid and do a simple backstitch to anchor the stitching at your stopping points.

Quilting

Most of my quilts combine machine quilting and some hand Appliquilting. For the machine work, I almost always use clear monofilament thread on the top and cotton thread that matches the backing fabric in the bobbin. I use machine quilting to add texture to the various buildings, such as straight lines for clapboards, or more intricate designs for brickwork or stonework. The horizontal quilting on the Pachena Point lighthouse (page 19) gives the feeling of siding much like the Trellis House in "Old Homesteads" (page 33), where I appliquéd each piece of siding separately. On the Portland Head lighthouse, the muslin sections were quilted in a brick design, giving it a texture that defines it from the rest of the buildings. I generally meander quilt in the background areas. That said, "Tattersall Lane" on page 58 uses Appliquilting exclusively. No additional machine quilting was added because the hand stitching adequately covered the entire piece.

Binding

When it comes to binding, there are many options and the choice is a personal one. Here's my favorite binding technique:

1. Cut binding strips 2½" wide and at least 10" longer than the perimeter measurement of the quilt. Sew the strips together end to end and press the seams open to reduce bulk.

2. Fold the long strip in half lengthwise, wrong sides together, and press well.

3. Beginning a few inches to the left of the bottom center and leaving at least 6" of binding as a tail, align the raw edges of the binding strip with the raw edges of the quilt top.

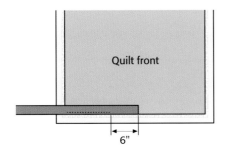

4. Stitch the binding strip to the edge of the quilt, using a ¼" seam allowance. Stitch to within ¼" of the corner, backstitch, remove the quilt from under the presser foot, and clip the threads.

5. Fold the unsewn binding strip in a miter, referring to the diagram. Begin stitching at the corner along the next edge of the quilt. Continue to stitch and miter corners on all four sides. Stop stitching along the final side of the quilt approximately 12" from where you began stitching. Backstitch and remove the quilt from the machine.

6. With your fingers, walk the two binding tails along the edge of the quilt until they meet. Hold both tails with the unstitched binding flat against the quilt edge; pin the tails together where they meet. Stitch the tails together at this point, from the folded edge to the raw edge.

7. Trim the tails to approximately ½" and finger-press the tails to each side of the seam.

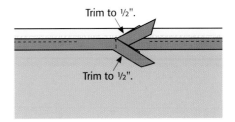

8. Sew the unstitched section of binding to the edge of the quilt. It should lie flat against the edge of the quilt, with no puckers.

9. Trim the excess batting and backing even with the raw edges of the quilt.

10. Turn the folded edge of the binding over the edge to the back, making sure the binding is filled with the edge of the quilt. Whipstitch in place, using thread to match the binding.

BEACONS OF LIGHT

Finished Quilt Size: 63" x 63"

Lighthouses have always seemed somewhat mysterious to me. They rarely serve their original function of warning seafarers of land anymore. A number of them have become private residences, while some are now museums. I have chosen five existing lighthouses to reproduce in this quilt, and on each one, I've used the blanket stitch to create a label containing the name of the lighthouse and the year it was constructed. If you have a particular favorite that I haven't included, you can adapt the designs given to emulate your desired lighthouse.

Notice how each lighthouse isn't appliquéd onto a traditional square or rectangular block. For this quilt, you'll first piece various-sized Ocean Waves blocks, appliqué the lighthouses onto irregular-shaped backgrounds, and then stitch them onto the pieced blocks.

Patchwork and Finishing Materials

Yardage is based on 42"-wide fabric.

- 3⅞ yards of unbleached muslin for Ocean Waves blocks
- 2¾ yards of assorted blue prints for Ocean Waves blocks and binding
- 4 yards of backing fabric
- 67" x 67" piece of batting
- Embroidery floss or size 8 pearl cotton: black, gold, gray, and off-white
- Template plastic
- Fine-point permanent marker

Appliqué Materials

Pachena Point

- ⅝ yard of hand-dyed dark blue fabric for background
- ½ yard of white or bleached muslin for lighthouse

- ⅛ yard of green fabric for grass
- Scraps of red, dark red, black, and gray for lighthouse
- Scrap of mottled charcoal for lighthouse base

Fisgard Island

- 4½" x 12" piece of textured muslin for lighthouse
- 6" x 17" piece of dark green fabric for grass
- 4" x 20" piece of rock print or dark textured fabric for island
- 3" x 18" piece of dark gray fabric for island
- 13" x 18" piece of hand-dyed light blue fabric for background
- 10" x 21" piece of hand-dyed medium blue fabric for background
- Scraps of 2 reds, black, brown, brick, gray crackle, and white crackle for lighthouse and light-keeper's house

Portland Head

- ⅔ yard (26" x 24") of pale blue mottled fabric for appliqué background
- ¼ yard of stone motif or dark gray fabric for land
- ⅛ yard of muslin for light-keeper's house
- 6" x 18" piece of pale gray mottled fabric for lighthouse
- Scraps of brick, soft red, black, dark gray, green, and medium blue for appliqués

Wood Islands

- ½ yard of blue mottled fabric for background
- Fat quarter of white crackle fabric for house
- 6" x 20" piece of green fabric for grass
- 4" x 16" piece of brown stripe for roofs
- Scraps of medium blue, dark gray, gray wood print, brick red, and red solid for appliqués

Brier Island

- ⅓ yard of mottled blue fabric for sky
- 6" x 12" piece of green fabric for grass
- Scraps of red, muslin, and light blue for lighthouse

Stars and Anchors

- ⅜ yard of gold fabric for anchors
- 6" x 15" strip of light gold fabric for star
- 6" x 15" strip of dark gold fabric for star
- 4" x 21" strip of navy blue fabric for star
- 2½" x 15" piece of dark red fabric for star
- 2½" x 15" piece of light red fabric for star

Cutting

From the muslin, cut:
1 rectangle, 17½" x 23⅛"
1 rectangle, 20¼" x 23⅛"
1 rectangle, 20½" x 26"
1 rectangle, 11⅞" x 20¼"
14 strips, 2⅞" x 42"; crosscut into 176 squares, 2⅞" x 2⅞"

5 strips, 4⅛" x 42"; crosscut into 35 squares, 4⅛" x 4⅛". Cut each square in half diagonally twice to yield 140 triangles.

From the assorted blue prints, cut:
14 strips, 2⅞" x 42"; crosscut into 176 squares, 2⅞" x 2⅞"

5 strips, 4⅛" x 42"; crosscut into 35 squares, 4⅛" x 4⅛". Cut each square in half diagonally twice to yield 140 triangles.

1 strip, 2½" x 19", from medium blue for water in Wood Islands block

Ocean Waves Block Construction

This quilt contains four Ocean Waves blocks, each of a different size. For the blocks you'll need to make a total of 352 blue-and-white triangle squares, plus use the individual blue and white triangles cut from the 4⅛" squares. The blocks are assembled in the same general manner, but each one uses a different number of triangles. Pay careful attention to the block diagrams for the number of triangle squares, triangles, and color placement.

To make the triangle squares, draw a diagonal line on one side of each 2⅞" white square from corner to corner. Layer each white square with a blue square, right sides together. Stitch ¼" on either side of the drawn line. Cut the squares apart on the drawn line. Press on top of the stitching to set the stitches and then press the resulting triangle squares open, with the seam allowance toward the blue fabric. Clip the dog ears.

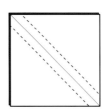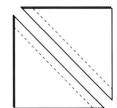

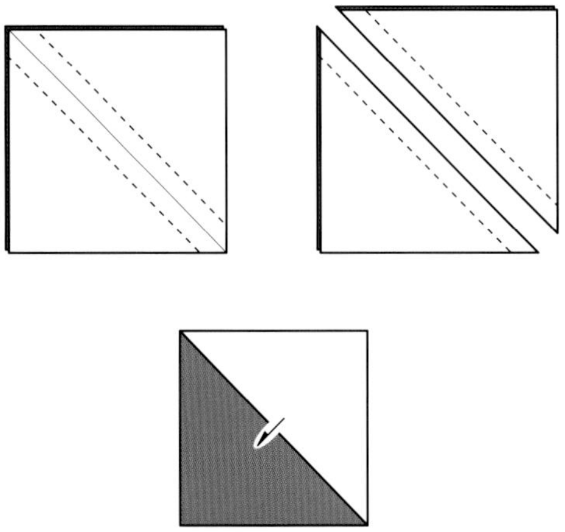

Make 352.

Pachena Point

1. Lay out the pieces for the Ocean Waves side borders. You'll need 18 triangle squares, eight white triangles, and four blue triangles for each border. Pay careful attention to the color placement and the direction the diagonal in each triangle square is pointing. Make two identical side border units.

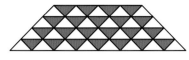

Side border unit.
Make 2.

2. In the same manner, make top and bottom border units. These are also identical to each other. You'll need 12 triangle squares, two white triangles, and six blue triangles for each border. Again, pay careful attention to the direction that the diagonal in each triangle square is pointing.

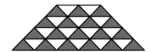

Top/bottom border unit.
Make 2.

3. Use 12 triangle squares, four white triangles, and four blue triangles for each corner unit. Note that the direction of the diagonals in the triangle squares changes from one half of each corner unit to the other. Make four corner units, two of each type.

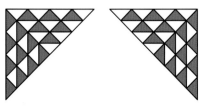

Corner units.
Make 2 of each.

4. Pin one of the Ocean Waves side borders to a long side of the 17½" x 23⅛" muslin rectangle, easing to fit if necessary. Stitch in place. Then sew the other side border to the opposite side of the muslin rectangle. Press the seams open to reduce bulk.

5. Sew the remaining two Ocean Waves borders to the rectangle, making sure the corners match. Press as before.

6. Attach the corner units to the block, making sure you sew the appropriate unit to each corner. Take care to match the seam allowances as you pin and then sew each corner in place. Press.

Pachena Point block

Fisgard Island

1. Lay out the pieces for the Ocean Waves side borders. You'll need six triangle squares, five white triangles, and seven blue triangles for each side border. Pay careful attention to the color placement and the direction the diagonal in each triangle square is pointing. Make two identical side border units.

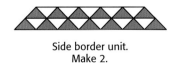

Side border unit.
Make 2.

2. In the same manner, make top and bottom border units. These are also identical to each other. You'll need seven triangle squares, eight white triangles, and six blue triangles for each border. Again, pay careful attention to the direction that the diagonal in each triangle square is pointing.

Top/bottom border unit.
Make 2.

3. Use two triangle squares, two white triangles, and two blue triangles for each corner unit. Note that the direction of the diagonals in the triangle squares changes from one half of each corner unit to the other. Make four corner units, two of each type.

Corner units.
Make 2 of each.

4. Referring to the directions for "Pachena Point" on page 19, sew the side borders and top and bottom borders to the 20¼" x 23⅛" muslin rectangle and attach the corner units. Press as before.

Fisgard Island block

Portland Head

1. Lay out the pieces for the Ocean Waves side borders. You'll need 21 triangle squares, nine white triangles, and five blue triangles for each side border. Pay careful attention to the color placement and the direction the diagonal in each triangle square is pointing. Make two identical side border units.

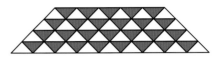

Side border unit.
Make 2.

2. In the same manner, make top and bottom border units. These are also identical to each other. You'll need 15 triangle squares, three white triangles, and seven blue triangles for each border. Again, pay careful attention to the direction that the diagonal in each triangle square is pointing.

Top/bottom border unit.
Make 2.

3. Use 12 triangle squares, four white triangles, and four blue triangles for each corner unit. Note that the direction of the diagonals in the triangle squares changes from one half of each corner unit to the other. Make four corner units, two of each type.

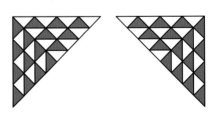

Corner units.
Make 2 of each.

4. Referring to the directions for "Pachena Point" on page 19, sew the side borders and top and bottom borders to the 20½" x 26" muslin rectangle, and attach the corner units. Press as before.

Portland Head block

Wood Islands

1. Lay out the pieces for the Ocean Waves side borders. You'll need six triangle squares and four blue triangles for each side border. Pay careful attention to the color placement and the direction the diagonal in each triangle square is pointing. Make two identical side border units.

Side border unit.
Make 2.

2. In the same manner, make top and bottom border units. These are also identical to each other. You'll need 15 triangle squares, seven white triangles, and three blue triangles for each border. Again, pay careful attention to the direction that the diagonal in each triangle square is pointing.

Top/bottom border unit.
Make 2.

3. Use 12 triangle squares, four white triangles, and four blue triangles for each corner unit. Note that the direction of the diagonals in the triangle squares changes from one half of each corner unit to the other. Make four corner units, two of each type.

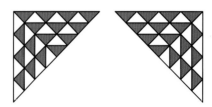

Corner units.
Make 2 of each.

4. Referring to the directions for "Pachena Point" on page 19, sew the side and top and

bottom borders to the 11⅞" x 20¼" muslin rectangle, and attach the corner units. Press as before.

Wood Islands block

Appliqué

Use the appliqué patterns on pages 1–5 of the foldout sheets to prepare plastic or freezer-paper templates for each pattern piece, referring to "Appliqué Templates" on page 11 as needed. Use the templates to cut out the fabric pieces, referring to the quilt photograph on page 16 and "Appliqué Materials" on pages 17–18 for the fabric colors.

Note: The Brier Island lighthouse is appliquéd onto the center of the quilt top after the other lighthouse blocks are assembled. For directions, see "Assembling the Quilt Top," step 4, on page 24.

Pachena Point lighthouse, located on Vancouver Island, British Columbia, is an example of the traditional eight-sided timber construction.

Pachena Point

1. Cut out the hand-dyed blue background piece and position on the Ocean Waves block. Notice that the appliqué background extends onto the blue and white triangles. Appliqué in place.

2. Referring to the quilt photograph, place the lighthouse motifs and the grass on the blue background. Appliqué the pieces in numerical order, overlapping them as necessary.

3. Using two strands of dark gray floss, stitch muntin bars on the windows, using an outline stitch or a stem stitch and following the dashed lines on the patterns. See "Embroidery" on page 13. Use two strands of off-white floss to stitch the muntin bars on the entryway door.

4. Referring to "Vines, Fences, Railings, and Casings" on page 12, prepare and appliqué window casings for the top and bottom windows.

5. Using a ruler, draw light pencil lines ½" apart on the white area of the lighthouse. The lines are drawn from seam to seam; they are not straight between the edges but appear to curve slightly. These are quilting lines to suggest siding (see photo).

Fisgard Island lighthouse is located in Victoria, British Columbia. It is now fully automated and still operating.

Fisgard Island

1. Sew the light blue sky and medium blue water pieces together along their straight edges, using a ¼" seam allowance. Press the seam allowance toward the water.

2. Appliqué the blue background unit to the Ocean Waves unit, referring to the quilt photograph. (You won't be able to complete the top part of the appliqué until this block has been sewn to the Pachena Point block because the appliqué background extends onto that block border.)

3. Position the lighthouse, the light-keeper's house, grass, and rock pieces on the appliqué background and stitch them in place in numerical order. In the quilt shown, I used the outline of the rocks in the printed fabric as the turn-under edge of my appliqué and you may wish to do the same.

4. Using two strands of off-white floss and a stem stitch (see page 13), embroider muntin bars on the windows and the fence in front of the lighthouse. Use two strands of black floss to stitch the doorknob and hinges as well as the railing at the top of the lighthouse. With one strand of gray floss, stitch the square architectural details below the black railing.

This rustic beauty still stands in Cape Elizabeth, Maine, where it has protected Portland and the surrounding area for over 200 years.

Portland Head

1. Appliqué the blue mottled sky background to the Ocean Waves block, referring to the quilt photograph for placement.

2. Arrange the additional appliqué background pieces (water, grass, and stones) on the background, overlapping pieces as necessary. Appliqué them in place.

3. Position the lighthouse and surrounding buildings on the background and stitch them in numerical order.

4. Using one strand of black floss and a stem stitch, stitch the railing at the top of the lighthouse tower and the pole on top of the roof. With two strands of off-white floss, stitch muntin bars on the window, again using a stem stitch.

5. Cut a narrow muslin strip, ⅝" to ¾" wide. Use this strip to make and appliqué the white fence, referring to "Vines, Fences, Railings, and Casings" on page 12.

The rustic Wood Islands lighthouse was build in the mid 1800s and still lights up the shoreline of Canada's Prince Edward Island province.

Wood Islands

1. Sew the medium blue 2½" x 19" strip between the light blue sky and green grass pieces, right sides together, using a ¼" seam allowance. Press the seam allowances toward the water.

2. Appliqué the three-piece background unit from step 1 to the Ocean Waves unit, referring to the quilt photograph for placement. (You cannot complete the appliqué at the bottom until this block has been joined to the Portland Head block below it because the appliqué background extends onto that block border.)

3. Position the lighthouse pieces on the background and appliqué them in numerical order.

4. Using two strands of off-white floss and a stem stitch, stitch the railings and muntin bars on the windows, following the dashed lines on the pattern pieces.

Assembling the Quilt Top

1. Sew the Pachena Point block to the top of the Fisgard Island block, matching points where the triangles meet. Make sure the top of the Fisgard Island appliqué is pinned out of the way. You can complete the appliqué once these two blocks have been joined. Press seam allowances to one side or open.

2. Sew the Wood Islands block to the top of the Portland Head block, matching the seam intersections of the triangles. Again, pin the unfinished appliqué out of the way before you sew the seam. Press seam allowances to one side or open. Complete the appliqué for the background of the Wood Islands lighthouse.

3. Sew the two sections together, with the Pachena Point and Fisgard Island lighthouses on the left and the Wood Islands and Portland Head lighthouses on the right. Press.

4. Appliqué the Brier Island lighthouse in the center of the assembled quilt. Stitch the mottled blue sky motif over the center portion of the quilt top, referring to the quilt photograph for placement. Then arrange the appliqué motifs on the background, overlapping pieces as necessary and stitching them in numerical order.

5. Using two strands of black floss and a stem stitch, embroider the railing near the top of the lighthouse. Use one strand of gray floss and a stem stitch to embroider the two lines on the lighthouse window. Use two strands of off-white floss and a stem stitch to embroider the platform on the left side of the lighthouse.

The original wooden Briar Island lighthouse in Nova Scotia was built in 1809, but burned down in 1994 and was replaced that same year with a concrete version.

Quilting and Finishing

1. Cut the backing fabric into two equal lengths. Remove the selvages and join the pieces to make a backing at least 67" x 67".

2. Layer the quilt backing, batting, and quilt top and baste the layers together. Hand or machine quilt as desired. The quilt shown is machine quilted. Follow the dashed lines on the lighthouse patterns for quilting architectural details. I quilted meandering patterns in the sky and patchwork backgrounds, and zigzag lines in the grassy areas.

3. Use the remaining blue fabric to make and attach the binding, referring to page14.

4. Use the appliqué patterns on the foldout sheets to prepare plastic or freezer-paper templates for the three star points and the large and small anchors, referring to "Appliqué Templates" on page 11 as needed. Be sure to mark the center line where appropriate.

5. From each of the light and dark gold fabrics, cut two strips, 3" x 15". Using a ¼" seam allowance, sew a light gold strip to a dark gold strip along the long edges. Repeat with the other two strips. Place the template for the gold star points on one of these units, aligning the center line on the template with the seam. Trace around the template and then cut out the star point ¼" outside the line. Repeat on the other gold strip set.

6. Sew the light and dark red 2½" x 15" strips together in the same manner and cut one red star point.

7. Cut one navy star point and three large and six small anchors from gold fabric.

8. Layer the star points, following the numerical order on the patterns and referring to the quilt photograph for placement. Also position the anchors. Referring to "Needle-Turn Appliquilting" on page 13, use gold or black embroidery floss or pearl cotton to sew the star points and anchors in place.

9. Cut muslin labels for each lighthouse and iron freezer paper to the back for ease in printing. Using a fine-point permanent marker, print the name of each lighthouse and the year it was built. If you prefer, you may embroider these details. Press the raw edges to the back of the labels and then remove the freezer paper. Sew the labels in place, using two strands of black floss and an overcast stitch as you did for the star points and anchors.

10. Label your finished quilt and enjoy it.

HOME SWEET HOME

Finished Quilt Size: 67½" x 67½"
Finished Block Size: 15" x 15"

Rustic appliqué, using an overcast stitch, made quick work of the traditional red Schoolhouse blocks for this project. (You'll find fewer pieces to cut and sew than for pieced Schoolhouse blocks.) The weeping willow trees are appliquéd in the same manner. I used many flannels in the quilt top. The white block backgrounds are flannel, as are the red-striped houses. The flannels work well with homespun plaids and stripes to create a comfy and cozy quilt, well suited to the project name, "Home Sweet Home."

After the appliquéd blocks, sashing, and borders are assembled, the project is machine quilted. The words, flowers, and vines in the sashing and border are added last, stitched through all layers with my Appliquilt method.

Materials

Yardage is based on 42"-wide fabric.

- 2½ yards of white solid for background
- ⅞ yard of green print for sashing
- 2 yards of dark green solid for border and willow trees
- 1¾ yards of red ticking for houses and binding
- 1 yard of dark red solid for sashing squares and letter appliqués
- ¼ yard of black plaid for roofs
- ¼ yard of medium green for vines
- Scraps or ⅛ yard each of 3 greens for leaves
- Scraps of beige, blue, gold, and red prints, plaids, and stripes for flowers
- 4½ yards of backing fabric
- 74" x 74" piece of batting
- Linen thread: natural
- Embroidery floss or pearl cotton: black, gold, and red
- Template plastic
- Fine-point permanent marker

Cutting

From the white solid, cut:
5 strips, 16" x 42"; crosscut into 9 squares, 16" x 16"

From the green print, cut*:
1 strip, 15½" x 42"; crosscut into 12 strips, 2½" x 15½"

6 strips, 2½" x 42"; crosscut each strip into 2 strips, 2½" x 15½"

*If you are using a directional fabric, cutting the sashing strips this way yields 12 sashing strips with horizontal stripes and 12 with vertical stripes so that all stripes will run in the same direction in the finished quilt.

From the dark red solid, cut:
1 strip, 2½" x 42"; crosscut into 16 squares, 2½" x 2½"

From the dark green solid, cut:
7 strips, 7" x 42"

From the red ticking, cut:
7 strips, 2½" x 42"

Making the Blocks

Use the appliqué patterns on pages 6 and 7 of the foldout sheets to prepare plastic or freezer-paper templates for each pattern piece, referring to "Appliqué Templates" on page 11 as needed. Use the templates to cut out the fabric pieces, referring to the quilt photograph on page 26 and "Materials" on page 27 for the fabric colors.

1. Arrange the motifs for one house on a 16" white background square. Be sure to place the roof motif so that it overlaps the seam allowances for the two chimneys. Using linen thread and the overcast stitch described on page 13, appliqué the chimneys first. Stitch around both sides and the top of the chimneys, but leave the bottom edge unsewn and do not turn under the seam allowances.

2. Appliqué the remaining pieces. Be sure to cut away the windows, leaving a ¼" seam allowance *inside* the windows' traced lines. To appliqué these edges, clip through the seam allowance at each window corner and turn under the edges along the marked lines.

3. Repeat steps 1 and 2 to complete five Schoolhouse blocks. Trim the completed blocks to 15½" x 15½", keeping the house motifs centered within the squares.

Schoolhouse block.
Make 5.

4. Center a tree on a 16" white background square. Stitch in place, using linen thread and an overcast stitch as above. Repeat to make four Willow Tree blocks. Trim the completed blocks to 15½" x 15½", keeping the tree motifs centered within the squares.

Willow Tree block.
Make 4.

Assembling the Quilt Top

1. Lay out the quilt blocks and sashing strips, alternating the two types of blocks as shown in the quilt plan on page 29. Place sashing strips and sashing squares between the block rows, making sure the design of the sashing fabric is oriented correctly if you're using a directional fabric.

2. Sew the units together in rows. You'll have four horizontal sashing rows and three horizontal block rows. Press all seam allowances toward the sashing strips.

3. Sew the rows together and press the seam allowances toward the sashing.

4. Sew three of the dark green border strips together end to end. Measure the length of the quilt top through the center, and from the long dark green strip, cut two border pieces to this length. Sew these borders to the sides of the quilt top and press the seam allowances toward the borders.

5. Sew the remaining four dark green strips together end to end in pairs. Measure the width of the quilt top, including the borders already in place. From each long border strip, cut a border to this length. Sew these borders to the top and bottom of the quilt top.

Quilting and Finishing

1. Cut the backing fabric into two equal lengths, remove the selvages, and sew the pieces together to make a quilt backing that is at least 74" x 74".

2. Layer the quilt backing, batting, and quilt top and baste the layers together. Hand or machine quilt as desired. The quilt shown is machine quilted. I quilted in the ditch along each sashing and border and meander quilted around the houses and trees. I also quilted in the large open area of the trees, mimicking the curves of the branches.

3. Use the red ticking strips to make and attach binding, referring to page 14 as needed.

4. Following the instructions for "Vines, Fences, Railings, and Casings" on page 12, prepare the flower, leaf, vines, and letters for needle-turn Appliquilting.

5. Referring to the quilt photograph for placement, pin your motifs to the quilt.

6. Using embroidery floss or pearl cotton in the colors of your choice, stitch the motifs to the quilt, stitching through all layers. Refer to "Needles and Thread" on page 10 and "Needle-Turn Appliquilting" on page 13 as needed.

7. Label your finished quilt and enjoy it.

Quilt plan

OLD HOMESTEADS

Finished Quilt Size: 57½" x 46½"

In this design, I combined traditional Log Cabin piecing with a variety of appliquéd houses. What a good use for my collection of building-materials fabrics—ones with wood-grain, bricks, or even crackled-paint patterns!

A series of appliquéd triangles, vines, and trellises lead your eye around the design. Another trick I like to use for adding movement to the design is to pick a particular fabric that stands out from the rest and use it in the Log Cabin piecing to catch the eye. Notice in this quilt that the triangle path follows along a bold printed plaid that coordinates colorwise, yet stands out from the other more subtle prints and plaids. I call this type of fabric a "zinger." A checkerboard, striped, or polka-dot fabric in a contrasting color are all possible choices for adding a zinger to your quilt.

Let your imagination loose and design a house or two of your own. Feel free to incorporate your own ideas—or even your own house—into my basic quilt design.

Materials

Yardage is based on 42"-wide fabric.

- ¾ yard of olive green for border
- ⅝ yard of high-contrast "zinger" for logs and binding
- ⅓ yard *each* of 3 dark plaids for backgrounds
- ¼ yard of black solid for background and windows
- ¼ yard *each* of 3 lights for backgrounds
- ⅛ to ¼ yard *each* of 4 different caramel browns for logs
- ⅛ to ¼ yard *each* of 6 different lights for logs
- ⅛ to ¼ yard *each* of 5 different grays for logs
- ⅛ to ¼ yard *each* of 5 charcoal grays for logs
- ⅛ to ¼ yard *each* of 3 white crackle or texture prints for houses
- ⅛ to ¼ yard *each* of 3 caramel wood-tone prints for houses, porches, roofs, and fences
- ⅛ yard of gray wood-tone print for window casings, doorjambs, and porches
- ⅛ yard of beige brick fabric for chimneys
- ⅛ yard *each* of 2 brown wood-tone prints for porches and tree trunks
- ⅛ yard of white texture for trellis house siding
- ¼ of dark green for trellis and vines
- Scraps of 6 to 8 assorted greens for tree leaves
- Scraps of assorted muted pastels for appliquéd triangles, flowers, and leaves
- 3⅛ yards of backing fabric
- 53" x 64" piece of batting

- Embellishments:

  Assorted round and square buttons for flower centers

  Moon- and flowerpot-shaped buttons

  ½ yard of twine for coiled rope

  Small wooden rake or other garden-implement ornament

  Dark green embroidery floss or size 8 pearl cotton
- Template plastic
- Fine-point permanent marker

Cutting

All strips are cut across the width of the fabric unless otherwise noted.

From the dark plaid, cut:
Block 1 background, 6½" x 13½"
Block 2 background, 9" x 12½"
Block 3 background, 12½" x 16½"

From the light fabrics, cut:
15 strips, 1½" x 42"
Block 4 background, 6½" x 13½"
Block 5 background, 2½" x 7½"
Block 5 background, 3½" x 9½"
Block 6 background, 10" x 13½"

From the caramel brown fabrics, cut:
9 strips, 1½" x 42"

From the charcoal gray fabrics, cut:
10 strips, 1½" x 42"
1 strip, 2½" x 13½"

From the zinger fabric, cut:
3 strips, 1½" x 42"
6 binding strips, 2½" x 42"

From the gray fabrics, cut:
6 strips, 1½" x 42"

From the black fabric, cut:
Block 5 background, 7½" x 7½"

From the white crackle fabric, cut:
5 strips, 1" x 13¾"

From the brown wood-grain fabric, cut:
5 strips, 1¼" x 13¾"
1 strip, 2" x 13¾"

From the beige brick fabric, cut:
2 strips, 1¾" x 13"

From the olive green, cut:
5 border strips, 4½" x 42"

Making the Log Cabin Blocks

For each block, sew the logs to the house background, which serves as the center of your Log Cabin block. Using a ¼" seam allowance, stitch the first log to the block center. The directions for where to begin attaching logs and whether to continue in a clockwise or counterclockwise direction are included with each set of house instructions.

1. Using either a dark or light strip (whichever the specific house directions call for), place it right sides together with the block background and stitch them together. Cut off the strip even with the edge of the block. Press the seam allowance toward the log fabric.

2. Turn the unit a quarter turn to the left or right as specified in the block directions, choose the appropriate color strip, and sew, trim, and press as before.

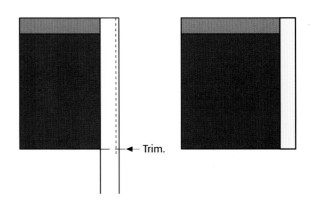

← Trim.

3. Continue turning the block and adding strips, making sure that two adjacent sides have light strips and the other two sides have dark strips, according to your block instructions. In most instances you will continue to add strips until three rounds of strips have been attached.

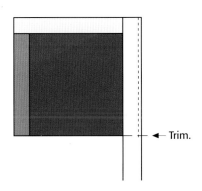

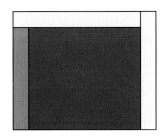

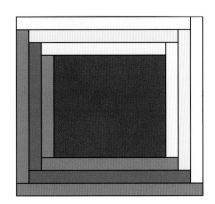

Block 1: Trellis House

1. Following the directions for making a Log Cabin block starting on page 32, begin by sewing a caramel strip to one long edge of the 6½" x 13½" dark background rectangle. Turn the block one quarter turn to the left (counterclockwise) and sew the same color

strip to the short edge of the block. Continue making counterclockwise quarter turns, and sew a light strip to the next two sides.

2. Continue adding logs in this manner until three rounds are complete. For this block, the dark logs should lie on the right and the bottom of the background and the light logs are on the left and the top. The block should measure 12½" x 19½".

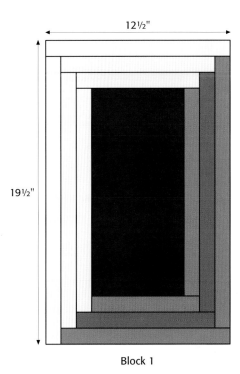

Block 1

3. Referring to "Appliqué Templates" on page 11, construct all the templates for the Trellis House, using the patterns on page 12 of the foldout sheets.

4. Referring to "Materials" on page 31 and the quilt photograph on page 30 for color ideas, use the templates to cut the following pieces: 12 right and 12 left siding pieces, three different eave pieces, one door, one window, the door and window casings, four roof siding pieces, and the underside of the roof. Note that the house in the quilt shown is made of individual pieces to represent siding. If you prefer, you can eliminate the individual pieces and simply cut one large piece for the

house. To give the illusion of siding, you could then quilt a series of parallel lines across the house.

5. Position the pieces, referring to the quilt photograph, and appliqué in place, following the instructions for "Traditional Appliqué" on page 12. Appliqué the siding first, overlapping the pieces as necessary. For edges that will be covered by other appliqués, leave them free (not turned under). Continue appliquéing the pieces in numerical order.

6. To make the trellis, refer to "Vines, Fences, Railings, and Casings" on page 12 and cut a ¾" x 42" strip from dark green fabric. Fold the strip in half lengthwise, wrong sides together, and stitch within a few threads of the raw edge by machine. Manipulate the seam so that it lies flat on one side. Press the strip well.

7. Cut the prepared green strip into the following lengths: one 7" strip, two 6¾" strips, two 6" strips, one 3½" strip, and one 2" strip. Arrange the strips, seam side down, on the right side of the house, referring to the pattern or quilt photograph. Appliqué the strips in place.

8. Referring to "Vines, Fences, Railings, and Casings," prepare window and door casings from the gray wood-tone fabric. Appliqué the pieces in place.

Block 2: Firewood House

1. Sew a light 1½"-wide strip along one long edge of the 9" x 12½" dark plaid rectangle. Trim, press the strip open, and turn the block counterclockwise a quarter turn. Sew a light strip to the next side of the block. Repeat, sewing a caramel strip to the next two sides of the block.

2. Repeat, adding three rounds of strips, with the light strips all on the right side and bottom of the dark rectangle, and the caramel strips on the left and top.

3. Add a final 1½"-wide light strip to the bottom of the block. The block should measure 15" x 19½".

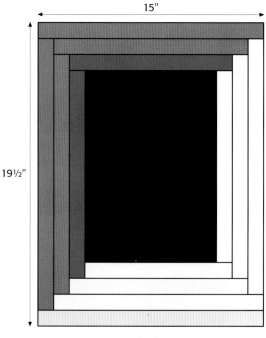

Block 2

4. Construct all the templates for the Firewood House, using the patterns on page 9 of the foldout sheets. Referring to "Materials" and the quilt photograph for color ideas, use the templates to cut the following pieces: three siding pieces, one chimney, one front porch, three upper roof strips, one porch roof, three log circles, one door, one window, and one door pediment. Also cut one ¾" x 6" strip of gray wood tone to make the window casings and one 1" x 27" strip of gray wood tone to make the doorjamb, porch floor, and porch posts.

Note: As with the Trellis House, you can make eight individual pieces of siding from a white crackle fabric, or you can simply cut one larger piece for the main part of the house. The edges of the house shown are not even, giving it a more realistic look. This look is not possible when cutting a single house piece.

5. Appliqué the pieces to the dark background using the traditional appliqué stitch. Overlap the pieces as necessary and stitch them in numerical order. When stitching the siding pieces, leave the top edge of each one free (not turned under) as it will be covered by the next piece of siding or roofing. You can also leave the left edges of the siding free, as they will be covered by the chimney.

6. Make the window, door, and porch pieces from the narrow gray wood-tone strips, referring to "Vines, Fences, Railings, and Casings" on page 12. Cut the narrower gray strip into two 1"-long pieces for the sides of the window and two 1½"-long pieces for the top and bottom of the window. Cut the wider strip into the following lengths: two 3½"-long pieces for the doorjamb, one 7½"-long piece for the porch floor, and two 6½"-long pieces for the porch posts. Position each in place and appliqué, turning under the raw ends that won't be covered by other appliqués.

Block 3: Log House

1. Sew a 1½"-wide light strip to one long edge of the 12½" x 16½" dark background rectangle. This will be the top of the block. Sew a second light strip to the one already attached to the background.

2. Rotate the block a quarter turn to the right (this is the opposite direction of the previous blocks), and add a light strip to the next side of the block. Continue rotating the unit clockwise, now adding charcoal strips to the bottom and other side of the block. For the next round, use light strips and charcoal strips, but for the third round, add the zinger fabric strips in place of the light strips. Complete the third round with charcoal strips on the bottom and right side.

3. To complete the block, add one more charcoal strip to the right side of the block only. The block should measure 23½" x 19½".

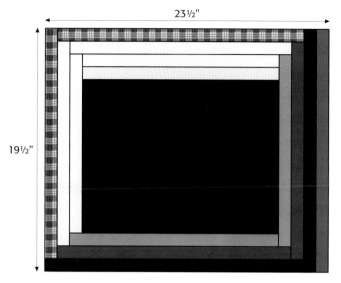

Block 3

4. Using the five 1¼" x 13¾" brown wood-grain strips and the five 1" x 13¾" white crackle strips, machine piece the log house. Sew the strips together along their long edges, beginning with a wood-grain strip and alternating colors. When you have three brown and three white strips sewn together, attach the 2" x 13¾" brown strip next. Then continue piecing, alternating the 1"-wide white strips with the 1¼"-wide brown strips.

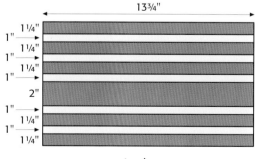

Log house

5. Construct the appliqué templates for the Log House, using the patterns on page 8 of the foldout sheets. Referring to "Materials" and the quilt photograph for color ideas, use the templates to cut the following pieces: one roof foundation, two roof logs, one door, two larger windows, one smaller window, one porch, and the stairs. Also cut one ¾" x 16" strip of light brown wood tone to make the window and door casings, a ¾" x 30" strip of gray wood tone to make the porch posts, and one 1" x 16" strip of medium brown wood tone to make the porch floor and hitching post.

6. Appliqué the pieces to the dark background in numerical order, starting with the strip-pieced house and overlapping the pieces as necessary.

7. Referring to "Vines, Fences, Railings, and Casings," use the ¾"-wide caramel wood-tone strip to make the window casings and doorjamb, the ¾"-wide gray wood-tone strip to make the porch posts, and the 1"-wide medium brown wood-tone strip to make the hitching post in front of the house. Appliqué these pieces in place.

Block 4: Trees

1. Sew a 1½"-wide caramel strip to one short side of the 6½" x 13½" light rectangle. This will be the top of the block.

2. Rotate the block a quarter turn to the right and add a caramel strip to the long side of the block. Continue rotating the block clockwise, now adding light strips to the bottom and right side of the block. Repeat until three

rounds of strips have been added: caramel on the top and left, and light on the bottom and right. The block should measure 12½" x 19½".

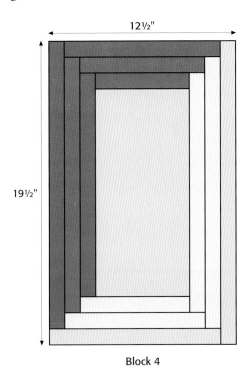

Block 4

3. Construct the tree trunk and leaf templates, using the patterns on page 8 of the foldout sheets. Using the templates, cut a large and small tree trunk from two different brown fabrics and 10 to 12 large leaves, 20 to 22 medium leaves, and 1 small leaf from assorted green fabrics. Position the pieces on the light background and appliqué in place.

Block 5: Shed

1. Sew the 2½" x 7½" light rectangle to the black 7½" square, using a ¼"-wide seam allowance. Press the seam allowance toward the square. Sew the 3½" x 9½" light rectangle to the unit so that the light rectangles are on the top and

left of the black square. Press as before. The pieced background unit should measure 9½" x 10½".

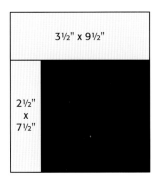

2. Sew a 1½"-wide gray strip to the 10½" right edge of the background unit. Rotate the unit a quarter turn to the left and add another gray strip to the bottom of the block. Repeat, sewing light strips to the next two sides of the block.

3. Add another round of strips in the same manner. On the third round, add gray strips to the right and bottom of the block as before. On the light side of the block, use the "zinger" fabric instead of more light strips.

4. Add three more sets of gray strips to the right and bottom of the block without adding any additional light strips to the block. The block should measure 18½" x 19½".

5. Construct the appliqué templates for the Shed, using the patterns on page 11 of the foldout sheets. Use the templates to cut the following pieces: nine shed siding pieces, seven roof siding pieces, one window, one chimney, two shed foundation blocks, four window casings, one fence post, and two fence rails.

6. Appliqué the pieces to the background in numerical order, overlapping them as needed. Don't turn under the top and left edges of the shed siding pieces or any edges of the windows. They will be covered by other pieces.

Block 6: Two-Story House

1. Sew the 2½" x 13½" charcoal strip to the 10" x 13½" light background rectangle. Rotate the block a quarter turn to the left and sew a 1½"-wide charcoal strip to the top of the rectangle. Sew a 1½"-wide light strip to the next two sides of the block.

2. Repeat, adding another round of dark and light 1½"-wide strips to the block, following the Log Cabin instructions on page 32. On the third round, use the "zinger" fabric on the light side of the block.

3. Sew three additional 1½"-wide charcoal strips to the left side of the block. The block should measure 19½" x 20".

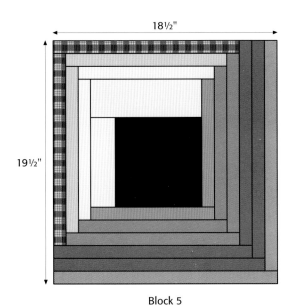

Block 5

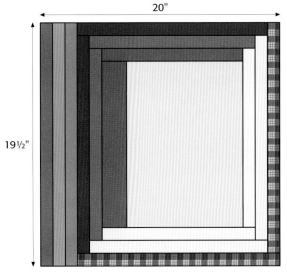

Block 6

4. Construct all templates for the Two-Story House, using the patterns on page 8 of the foldout sheets. Use the templates to cut the following pieces: nine front and nine side siding pieces, five eaves pieces, one house roof and one porch roof, the window and door pediments, one porch floor, one back roof, two trees, the windows and doors, and front eaves. Also cut one ¾" x 42" strip of light brown wood tone to make the window casings, doorjamb, porch railings, and porch posts.

5. Appliqué the pieces to the background in numerical order, overlapping the pieces as needed. Be sure to overlap siding so that the corner of the house measures 8" from the bottom to the roof line.

6. Use the ¾"-wide strip of brown wood tone to make the porch posts and railings, window casings, and doorjamb referring to "Vines, Fences, Railings, and Casings."

Assembling the Quilt Top

1. Lay out the blocks in two horizontal rows. Blocks 1, 2, and 3 make up the top row; blocks 4, 5, and 6 form the bottom row. Sew the blocks together in horizontal rows and then sew the two rows together. Press the seam allowances to one side. The quilt top should measure 50" x 38½".

2. Measure the length of your quilt top and cut two olive green border strips to this length. Sew the borders to the sides of the quilt top and press the seam allowances toward the borders.

3. Measure the width of the quilt, including the side borders. It should be approximately 58" wide. Sew the three remaining olive green border strips together end to end. From this long strip, cut two borders to fit your quilt. Sew the borders to the top and bottom of the quilt and press the seam allowances toward the borders.

Quilt plan

Quilting and Finishing

1. Cut the backing fabric into two equal lengths, remove the selvages, and sew the pieces together to make a quilt backing that is at least 51" x 62".

2. Layer the quilt backing, batting, and quilt top and baste the layers together. Hand or machine quilt as desired. The quilt shown is machine quilted. I quilted a straight line through the vertical center of each log, between the siding on the houses, and outlined the trees and leaves. I quilted in the ditch on the Log House and meandered in the exposed parts of the Log Cabin backgrounds.

3. Use the 2½"-wide "zinger" fabric strips to make and attach the binding, referring to page 14 as needed.

4. Cut two sections of vines, one ¾" x 32" and one ¾" x 55". They do not have to be continuous pieces, since flowers or leaves could cover the seaming. Prepare the vines, referring to "Vines, Fences, Railings, and Casings," and Appliquilt them to the front of the quilt, referring to the photograph on page 30 for placement and page 12 for stitching instructions.

5. Make templates for the flowers, leaves, and triangles for the quilt border, using the patterns on the foldout sheets. Use them to prepare 47 triangles and 17 flowers from various pastel fabrics and 24 green leaves. Appliquilt these shapes to the quilt top, referring to the photograph for placement ideas.

6. Cut seven strips, ¾" x 42", from a caramel fabric for the fences. Referring to "Vines, Fences, Railings, and Casings," stitch the fences to the border.

7. Add embellishments to the quilt as desired. I found a flowerpot button that I sewed to the porch on block 6. Then using three strands of dark green floss, I embroidered 8 to 10 straight stitches to look like a potted plant. Sew buttons to the centers of the Appliquilted flowers. Add a moon button to the Trees block. I also stitched a coiled piece of twine to the front of the Shed and a small bamboo rake to the Log House.

8. Label your finished quilt and enjoy it.

Barn Raising

Finished Quilt Size: 54½" x 46½"

Barns are true American icons, but sadly they are vanishing from the countryside. For this quilt, I've preserved a bit of Americana by appliquéing my interpretation of five different styles of barns.

Two sizes of Nine Patch blocks as well as Star blocks and small squares are pieced together to frame and connect the barns. Select a variety of fat quarters in rich autumn tones of gold, red, brown, and green for piecing these units so that you'll have a good assortment of colors and textures, which makes for an interesting quilt. Save the leftovers to piece the quilt backing as I did.

In a few places in the quilt shown, you'll see that some of the Nine Patch blocks have been cut off or a random piece of fabric has been inserted into the sashing to make it fit. That's because I made up the quilt as I went along, working in a primitive style. To ensure that the cutting and piecing directions would work precisely for you, we've slightly altered the background block sizes. If you cut and sew accurately, you'll have a folk-art style quilt without having to fudge any of the seams!

Materials

Yardage is based on 42"-wide fabric.

- 10 fat quarters of assorted reds, greens, golds, browns, grays, and tans for Nine Patch blocks and sashing squares
- 5 fat quarters of assorted golds, red-browns, and caramels for appliqué backgrounds
- 4 fat quarters of assorted reds for barns
- ⅝ yard of black solid for windows, doors, and binding
- 1 fat quarter of gray wood-tone print for Pine Ridge Ponies roof
- ¼ yard of white crackle for fences, casings, and signposts
- ⅛ yard *each* or scraps of 3 dark gray textures for roofs and siding
- ⅛ yard *each* or scraps of 3 gray wood-tone prints for barns
- ⅛ yard *each* or scraps of 3 black plaids and stripe for roofs
- ⅛ yard or scraps of dark brown solid and textures for barn roof
- ⅛ yard or scrap of beige brick print for barn foundation
- ⅛ yard or scrap of dark red stripe for barn
- ⅛ yard or scrap of light brown wood-tone print for barn details
- ⅛ yard each or scraps of light and dark gray mottled prints for silos
- ⅛ yard or scraps of beige textures for door and path

- ⅛ yard or scrap of bleached muslin for signs
- ⅛ yard or scraps of pink for pig and cow
- ⅛ yard or scraps of white-with-black polka-dot print for chicken
- ⅛ yard or scrap of black-and-white cow print for cow
- ⅛ yard or scrap of cheddar solid for Star blocks and sun
- 2⅜ yards of backing fabric
- 51" x 64" piece of batting
- Embroidery floss or pearl cotton: black, green, gold, bright orange, and yellow
- Embellishments:
    2 large and 2 small pumpkin buttons
    6 small red buttons
    2 chicken buttons (1 black and 1 white)
    1 cow button
    1 milk-bottle button
    1 preprinted American flag (3" x 4")
- Template plastic
- Fine-point permanent marker

Cutting

From the assorted gold, red-brown, and caramel fat quarters for backgrounds, cut:
1 rectangle, 16½" x 18½"
2 rectangles, 12½" x 18½"
1 rectangle, 12½" x 15½"
1 rectangle, 12½" x 13½"
1 strip, 1½" x 18½"

From the assorted fat quarters for Nine Patch blocks, cut:
42 strips, 2½" x 21"; crosscut the strips into 330 squares, 2½" x 2½"
18 strips, 1½" x 21"; crosscut the strips into 234 squares, 1½" x 1½"

From 1 of the gold fat quarters, cut:
8 squares, 2½" x 2½"
2 squares, 3¼" x 3¼"

From the cheddar solid, cut:
2 squares, 2½" x 2½"

From 1 of the red fat quarters, cut:
4 squares, 2⅞" x 2⅞"
2 squares, 3¼" x 3¼"

From the black solid, cut:
6 binding strips, 2½" x 42"

Making the Barn Blocks

Use the appliqué patterns on the foldout sheets to prepare plastic or freezer-paper templates for each pattern piece, referring to "Appliqué Templates" on page 11 as needed. Use the templates to cut out the fabric pieces, referring to the quilt photograph on page 40 and "Materials" on page 41 for color ideas.

Pine Ridge Ponies

1. Using the patterns on page 9 of the foldout sheets for the "Pine Ridge Ponies" barn, prepare all the pieces for appliqué: right, center, and left barn from red; right, center, and left cupola from red; right, center, and left barn roof and cupola roof from gray; windows from black solid; door from light brown wood tone; and trees from two different dark greens.

Pine Ridge Ponies is an example of a round barn, many of which are located in the midwestern United States.

2. Arrange the appliqués on a 12½" x 18½" background rectangle. Appliqué the pieces to the background in numerical order, overlapping them as needed. Leave the left side of the barn and both roofs unsewn for now. You'll add the tree later after attaching the Nine Patch border.

3. Cut a ½" x 12" strip and a ¾" x 24" strip from the white crackle fabric. Referring to "Vines, Fences, Railings, and Casings" on page 12, use the ½"-wide strip to make and appliqué casings for the smaller windows in the cupola. Use the ¾"-wide strip to make and appliqué casings for the larger barn windows and doorjamb.

Maple Leaf Acres

1. Using the patterns on page 9 of the foldout sheets for the "Maple Leaf Acres" barn, prepare all the pieces for appliqué: upper barn, lower barn, and silo from three different grays; silo roof from dark brown; roof tiles from two different dark browns; barn foundation from beige brick print; door opening and windows from black solid; barn door from beige; barn-door tracker from light brown wood-tone; and tree from dark green.

2. Arrange the appliqués on a 12½" x 18½" background rectangle. Appliqué the pieces to the background in numerical order, overlapping them as needed. Note that the tree cannot be completely appliquéd until the sashing has been added to the block. Leave the left edge free for now.

3. Using two strands of black floss, take five straight stitches evenly spaced from the top of the hanging door to the bottom of the wood-tone tracker strip. Using three strands of green floss, embroider plants as shown to indicate a field on the background fabric.

Come up at A and down at B.
Repeat, coming up at A, down at C,
and again from A to D.

Pumpkin Hollow

1. Using the patterns on page 10 of the foldout sheets for the "Pumpkin Hollow" barn, prepare all the pieces for appliqué: barn, barn sides, and small door from red (I used a stripe for these pieces and cut the barn and one side with the stripe running vertically, and the other side and upper door with the stripe running horizontally); window and large door from black solid; roofs from tan or brown; and the path from tan.

Maple Leaf Acres is a weathered gray barn with a brick foundation and round silo.

Pumpkin Hollow is a wooden barn with a traditional gabled roof.

2. Arrange the appliqués on the 12½" x 13½" background rectangle. Appliqué the pieces to the background in numerical order, overlapping them as needed.

3. Cut a ¾" x 18" strip from the white crackle fabric. Referring to "Vines, Fences, Railings, and Casings," use this strip to make the X on the small door and to frame the large door, small door, and window. Refer to the photograph for placement.

4. Cut a ½" x 7" strip from the light brown wood-tone fabric. Working in the same manner as for the door frames, cut four bench legs 1" long and a bench seat 2½" long. Position the bench to the left of the large door and appliqué in place.

Spring Meadow Farm

1. For the barn foundation, cut a 3½" x 11" dark gray strip. For the barn itself, cut a 5" x 11" red strip. Sew these two pieces together along their long edges and then prepare this piece for appliqué.

2. Using the patterns on page 11 of the foldout sheets for the "Spring Meadow Farm" barn, prepare the following pieces for appliqué: red barn loft and barn door, black roof tiles, black windows and door opening, and white crackle pediment for the loft window.

Spring Meadow Farm is a red barn with a round or Gothic roof.

3. Arrange the motifs on the 12½" x 15½" background rectangle. Appliqué the pieces to the background in numerical order, overlapping them as needed. Overlap the roof tiles, starting at the lower-left edge of the roof until you reach the top of the roof. Then begin again at the lower right and work to the top center of the roof. The uppermost left and right tiles should meet at the top of the roof.

4. Cut a ¾" x 16½" strip of white crackle fabric. Use this strip to encase the large window on four sides and to make the diagonal pieces. Likewise, cut a ¾" x 7" strip of light brown wood tone to make the barn-door tracker strip above the barn doors.

5. Using two strands of black floss, stitch short, straight vertical stitches between the top of the hanging door and the wood-tone tracker strip above it. Using two strands of gold floss, stitch long, straight stitches from the lower portion of the loft window to resemble hay.

Sunshine Dairy

1. For the barn foundation, cut a 3½" x 11½" gray wood-tone strip. For the barn itself, cut a 9" x 11½" gray wood-tone strip. (In the quilt shown, I cut the foundation with the grain running horizontally and the barn with the grain running vertically.) Sew these two strips together along their long edge and then prepare this piece for appliqué.

Sunshine Dairy features a gambrel roofline and a classic round silo.

2. Using the patterns on page 10 of the foldout sheets for the "Sunshine Dairy" barn, prepare the following pieces for appliqué: silo from light gray, barn loft from dark red, windows from black solid, barn and silo roofs from black check or plaid, barn sign from muslin, and sun from cheddar solid.

3. Arrange the motifs on the 16½" x 18½" background rectangle. Appliqué the pieces to the background in numerical order, overlapping them as needed.

4. Cut a ¾" x 8" strip of white crackle fabric and use it to make appliqué casings around the square window.

5. Cut a ½" x 15" strip from brown wood-tone fabric. Cut this strip into six equal lengths. Use these pieces to make fence posts, spaced approximately 2½" to 2¾" apart. Appliqué the fence posts in place. Using two strands of black floss, backstitch four equally spaced horizontal lines between all fence posts. At each ½" interval, place a very short perpendicular stitch to resemble barbed wire.

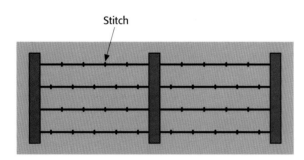

Embroider the barbed-wire fencing.

6. Using a running stitch with two strands of bright orange floss, stitch the Sunshine Dairy sign to the barn. Using two strands of the bright orange floss, stitch long stitches around the sun you have appliquéd over the left end of the sign. Use two strands of yellow floss to make long stitches around the sun, placing the stitches between the bright orange ones.

Making the Star Blocks

1. Draw a diagonal line on the wrong side of the two 3¼" gold squares. Layer each of them right sides together with a red 3¼" red square. Sew the layered squares together, stitching ¼" from each side of the drawn lines. Cut the squares apart on the drawn lines and press the resulting triangle squares open, pressing the seam allowances toward the red print. Trim the dog ears.

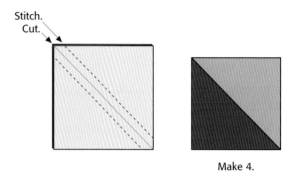

Make 4.

2. Pair each of the triangle squares from step 1 with a 2⅞" red square. Layer them right sides together. Using a ruler and pencil, draw a diagonal line that runs in the opposite direction of the seam line. Stitch ¼" from each side of the drawn lines. Cut the squares apart on the drawn lines, trim the dog ears, and press. You now have eight star-point units.

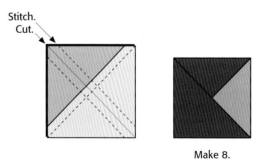

Make 8.

3. Using four star-point units, four 2½" gold squares, and one 2½" cheddar square, arrange the pieces for one Star block. Sew the pieces together into three rows. Press the

center-row seams toward the solid cheddar square. Press the two outer-row seams toward the red squares. Sew the three rows together, nestling the seams that have been pressed in opposite directions. Repeat to make a second Star block.

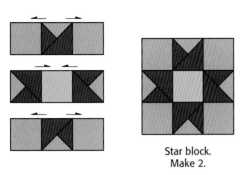

Star block.
Make 2.

Making the Sashing and Border Blocks

The sashing is pieced in sections of small Nine Patch blocks and rows of 2" finished squares. Each block has its own unique sashing requirements, which will enable you to assemble the quilt in rows.

1. Using the 1½" assorted-color squares, select four squares of one color and five of another. Arrange the squares as shown to form a Nine Patch block. Sew the squares together in rows and then sew the rows together. Press the seams in alternating directions from row to row. The block should measure 3½" square, including the seam allowances. Repeat to make 26 of these small Nine Patch blocks for the sashing.

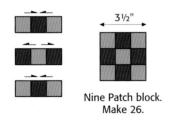

Nine Patch block.
Make 26.

2. Using the 2½" assorted-color squares, piece 30 larger Nine Patch blocks for the border in the same manner as in step 1. These blocks should measure 6½" square, including the seam allowances.

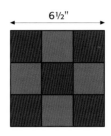

Nine Patch block.
Make 30.

3. You'll need two additional segments for the border. Select two 2½" squares of one color and one 2½" square of a contrasting color. Sew them together in a row to resemble one row of a Nine Patch block. Repeat to make a second unit. You can use the same colors or two different ones

Make 2.

4. Using the remaining 2½" assorted squares, make four rows of nine squares each. Sew these rows together in pairs. Also make one row of six squares and three rows of three squares each as shown.

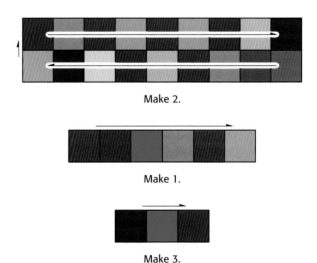

Make 2.

Make 1.

Make 3.

BARN RAISING

Assembling the Quilt Top

1. Sew one of the long (4½" x 18½") strips of squares to the left side of the Maple Leaf Acres block. The completed block should measure 16½" x 18½".

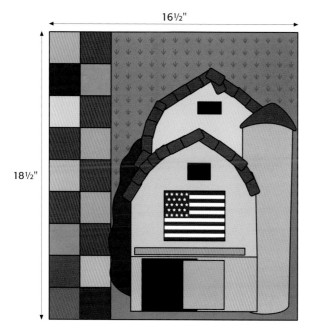

2. Sew four of the small Nine Patch blocks together in a row and then sew the row to the bottom of the Pumpkin Hollow block. Sew the six-square strip from step 4 on page 46 to the top of the block. Finally, sew the remaining long strip of squares to the left side of the block.

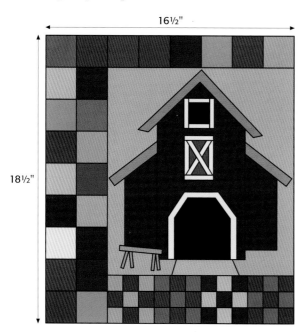

3. Arrange the two Star blocks and three short rows of sashing squares in a vertical column, alternating the units. Sew these pieces together, pressing the seam allowances toward the squares. Then make two rows of small Nine Patch blocks, each with six blocks. Sew these rows to the left and right sides of the star unit. Press the seam allowances toward the Nine Patch blocks. This block should measure 12½" x 18½".

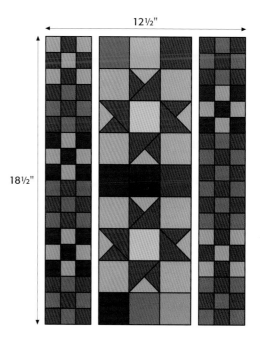

4. Use the remaining small Nine Patch blocks to make two rows of five blocks each. Sew one row to the right side of the Spring Meadow block. Press the seam allowances toward the barn. Then sew the other row to the top of the block. Press in the same manner. To complete the block, sew the 1½" x 18½" strip of background fabric (red-brown, gold, or caramel) to the right side of

the block. Press the seam allowances toward this strip. The completed block should measure 16½" x 18½".

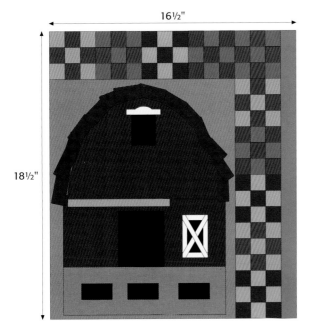

16½"

18½"

5. Lay out the six blocks in two horizontal rows, with the Pine Ridge Ponies, Maple Leaf Acres, and Pumpkin Hollow blocks in the top row, and the Star, Spring Meadow, and Sunshine Dairy blocks in the bottom row. Sew the blocks together into two rows and then join the rows. Press.

6. To make the top and bottom Nine Patch borders, sew together two rows of seven blocks each. Then add one three-square strip to the end of each border. Press the seam allowances to one side and attach the borders to the top and bottom of the quilt. In the same manner, assemble two side borders by sewing together eight Nine Patch blocks for each border. Press the seam allowances to one side and attach the borders to the sides of the quilt.

Quilt assembly

BARN RAISING

7. After the borders have been attached, complete the tree appliqués on Pine Ridge Ponies and Maple Leaf Acres.

Quilting and Finishing

1. Cut the backing fabric into two equal lengths, remove the selvages, and sew the pieces together to make a quilt backing that is at least 52" x 60".

2. Layer the quilt backing, batting, and quilt top and baste the layers together. Hand or machine quilt as desired. The quilt shown is machine quilted. I quilted diagonal lines through the Nine Patch blocks and squares, and meander quilted in the background of the appliqué blocks. I added architectural details in the barns, such as outlining doors and windows or quilting along the lines of the wood-grain fabrics to emphasize them.

3. Use the 2½"-wide black solid strips to make and attach the binding, referring to page 14 as needed.

4. After the quilting is complete, add the appliquéd fences, using the white crackle fabric and referring to "Vines, Fences, Railings, and Casings" on page 12. Use the quilt photograph on page 40 for placement ideas. Make a label for the Pine Ridge Ponies, Maple Leaf Acres, and Spring Meadow farms, using muslin fabric and the patterns on the pullout sheets.

5. Using two strands of black floss, stitch the words "Pumpkin Hollow" on the appropriate block. Use the green floss and the stem stitch to embroider vines for the pumpkins on this block. Sew the two small pumpkin buttons to the bench and the two larger pumpkin buttons to the upper-right corner where the vines have been stitched.

6. Sew the chicken button to the loft of the Spring Meadow barn. On the quilt shown, another chicken button was added to the sashing. Finally, use black floss to Appliquilt the cow, pig, and chicken in the lower-left corner of the quilt border, using the patterns on page 10 of the foldout sheet and referring to the overcast stitch described on page 13.

7. Label your finished quilt and enjoy it.

CALL TO WORSHIP

Finished Quilt Size: 54½" x 50½"

While the churches in this quilt have some similarities, such as steeples, notice that each one has its own unique architecture. To tie all of the different-shaped blocks and various-style churches together, I used the same light blue background for each and appliquéd twining vines along the checkerboard sashing and borders.

Once again, I used stone, wood-grain, and other building-material fabrics to help bring the appliqué to life. To further accentuate the architecture of the buildings, I used quilting patterns to suggest the look of clapboards, bricks, and stonework. The Round Church is a good example of how quilting can be used to create contrast between two sections of the same building. The center is closely quilted in a casual bricklike design, while the side sections are quilted with the same design but on a larger scale. Even though all three sections of the church are made from the same fabric, the separate sections are clearly defined.

Materials

Yardage is based on 42"-wide fabric.

- 1⅜ yards of light blue fabric for block backgrounds
- 1⅜ yards of gold solid for sashing, border, and binding
- 1⅛ yards of white-on-white ticking for Country Church
- ⅞ yard of cream solid for sashing and border
- ⅜ yard of stone print for Stone Church
- ¼ yard of bleached muslin for Round Church
- ¼ yard or fat quarter of white-on-white stripe for Pillar Church
- ⅛ yard of mottled black print for Stone Church roofs
- ⅛ yard of dark charcoal print for Round Church roofs
- ⅛ yard of patterned dark gray for Country Church roofs
- Scrap or ⅛ yard of dark taupe print for Country Church windows
- Scrap or ⅛ yard of light taupe print for Country Church steeple trim
- Scrap or ⅛ yard of brick print for Pillar Church roof
- Scrap or ⅛ yard of multicolor marble print for windows
- Scrap or ⅛ yard of medium gray texture for windows
- Scrap or ⅛ yard of mottled white print for steeple, window casings, and porch posts
- Scrap or ⅛ yard of off-white tone-on-tone print for window casings and ledges

- Scrap or ⅛ yard of pale gray rock print for pathways
- Scrap or ⅛ yard of bright print on black background for windows
- Scrap or ⅛ yard of caramel wood-tone print for doors
- Scrap or ⅛ yard of white crackle print for steeple trim
- ¼ yard of dark green print for vines
- Scraps or ⅛ yard each of 10 different green prints (or enough to equal ½ yard) for leaves and shrubs
- 1⅝ yards of backing fabric
- 54" x 58" piece of batting
- Embroidery floss or pearl cotton: dark brown, ecru, gold, gray, and dark green
- Template plastic
- Fine-point permanent marker

Cutting

From the light blue fabric, cut:
1 square, 20½" x 20½"
1 rectangle, 14½" x 22½"
1 rectangle, 20½" x 24½"
1 rectangle, 12½" x 24½"

From the cream solid, cut:
11 strips, 2½" x 42"

From the gold solid, cut:
17 strips, 2½" x 42"

Making the Church Blocks

Use the appliqué patterns on pages 11–14 of the foldout sheets to prepare plastic or freezer-paper templates for each pattern piece, referring to "Appliqué Templates" on page 11 as needed. Use the templates to cut out fabric pieces, referring to the quilt photograph on page 50 and "Materials" on page 51 for fabric colors.

The Round Church features a large round stained glass window and three Gothic arched windows.

Round Church

1. Arrange the motifs for the Round Church and the tall shrubs on either side of the church on the 20½" blue background square, referring to the quilt photograph for placement. (The remaining shrubs won't be appliquéd until the quilt is assembled.) Pin them in place.

2. Appliqué the motifs in numerical order, overlapping them as needed.

    Note: Leave the left edge of the tall tree on the left side of the church unstitched so that you can slip the shrubbery appliqués under the tree once the quilt is assembled. Also, you do not need to turn under the bottom edge of the church or its door because these pieces will be enclosed in the seam allowance at the bottom of the block when the sashing is added to the block.

3. The circular window can easily be reverse appliquéd. Simply cut the bright-print circle and place it beneath the light casing fabric. Cut out the inner circle, leaving a ⅛" seam allowance, and turn the edges under, appliquéing the casing to the bright fabric. Then stitch the window unit to the church facade.

4. Using all six strands of dark brown floss and straight stitches, add hinges and door handles to the double doors.

The Stone Church also features stained glass and two rows of arched windows.

The simple white clapboards and plain windows are a good foil for the dramatic steeple of this Country Church.

Stone Church

1. Arrange the motifs for the Stone Church on the 14½" x 22½" blue background block, referring to the quilt photo for placement.

2. Appliqué the motifs in numerical order, overlapping them as needed. You may find it easier to reverse appliqué the interior parts of the curved windows. Place the "glass" fabric beneath the white window-frame fabric, and cut out the interior window shape, leaving a ⅛" seam allowance. Turn under the window-frame fabric and appliqué it to the glass fabric.

   Note: The stone pathway and green shrubbery in front of and on the side of the church will be appliquéd after the sashing and borders have been added.

3. Using one strand of ecru floss and a stem stitch (see page 13), stitch the muntin bars on the rectangular windows. Using two strands of gray floss and the stem stitch, stitch the cross to the top of the steeple.

4. Referring to "Vines, Fences, Railings, and Casings" on page 12 and the quilt photo for placement, make and appliqué the porch posts, the window ledges on the lower row of rectangular windows, muntin bars on the large window, and the eaves along the lower roof line of the steepled section and the porch roof.

Country Church

When cutting out the motifs for this church, take care to watch the direction of the stripes. The arrows on the patterns indicate the direction that the stripes should run to give you good contrast between the various building parts. The difference is subtle, but noticeable.

1. Arrange the motifs for the Country Church on the 20½" x 24½" blue background block, referring to the quilt photograph for placement. All the shrubbery is added after the quilt top has been assembled.

2. Appliqué the motifs in numerical order, overlapping them as needed.

3. Referring to "Vines, Fences, Railings, and Casings," cut a ½" x 3" strip from light taupe to make the narrower strip below the steeple window and cut a ¾" x 3" strip to make the wider strip above the window.

4. Using one strand of ecru floss and a stem stitch, sew the muntin bars on the windows. Using three strands of dark brown floss and a stem stitch, add decorative lines on the door and stitch a French knot for the doorknob (see page 13).

Brick columns support the portico and the steeple on this white Pillar Church.

Pillar Church

As with the Country Church, plan the direction that you want the stripes to run to give you good contrast between the various building parts.

1. Arrange the motifs for the Pillar Church on the 12½" x 24½" blue background block, referring to the quilt photograph for placement. The brick sections that flank the center of the church are made of two large rectangles (one on each side of the center portion of the church). Then narrow white pillars are appliquéd over the rectangles so that only narrow portions of brick remain visible. Again, the shrubbery is added after the quilt is assembled.

2. Appliqué the motifs in numerical order, overlapping them as needed. For the stained-glass window and the smaller white triangle (the portico roof), it is easiest to reverse appliqué these shapes. For instance, place the colored-print fabric under the light gray casing fabric; cut out the interior circle, leaving a ⅛" seam allowance; and then appliqué the gray fabric onto the colored print. Appliqué the black portico roof over the white triangle in the same manner, then appliqué these units to the church.

3. Using one strand of gray floss and a stem stitch, sew the muntin bars on the rectangular windows. Using two strands of gold floss, make a small cross-stitch on the door for a knob.

Assembling the Quilt Top

As you assemble the quilt top, press the checkerboard sashing seam allowances toward the appliqué blocks. Press the outer-border seam allowances away from the appliqué blocks.

1. Sew nine of the 2½"-wide cream strips to a 2½"-wide gold strip. Press the seam allowances toward the gold strips. Crosscut the strip sets into 135 units, 2½" wide.

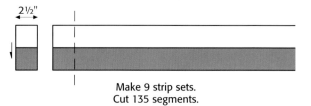

2½"

Make 9 strip sets.
Cut 135 segments.

2. Sew the units from step 1 together to make checkerboard sashing. You will need a 10-unit strip, an 11-unit strip, and a 12-unit strip. Make sure to position the colors as shown so that once the quilt is assembled, the checkerboard design will flow seamlessly around the quilt.

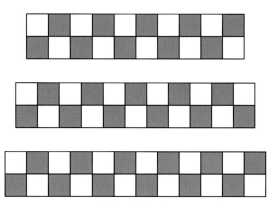

Make 1 of each.

CALL TO WORSHIP

3. Sew the 10-unit sashing to the right side of the Round Church block, with a gold square in the upper-left corner of the strip.

4. Using six of the remaining two-square units, sew them together end to end, alternating colors. Sew this strip to the bottom of the Round Church block, making sure that the colors alternate at the bottom-right corner of the block.

5. Sew the Country Church block to the bottom of the unit constructed in step 4 to complete one row of the quilt.

6. Sew the 11-unit sashing strip to the bottom of the Stone Church block.

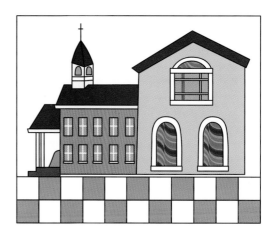

7. Sew the 12-unit sashing strip to the right side of the Pillar Church block.

8. The sashing on the left side of the Pillar Church is wider than the other sashing units. To make this sashing, sew one of the remaining 2½"-wide cream strips to a 2½"-wide gold strip. Press the seam allowances toward the gold strip. Then cut the final cream strip in half so you have a piece 2½" x 21". Do the same with a gold strip and with the strip set you just made. Using the partial-length strips, make one of each of the strip sets as shown below.

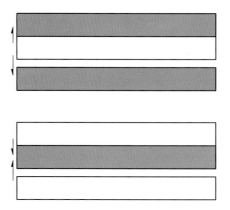

9. Crosscut the strip sets from step 8 into 2½"-wide segments. Using six segments from each strip set, sew the segments together along their long edges, alternating them to create

the checkerboard pattern. Sew this unit to the left of the Pillar Church so that the top edge has cream squares on the outside edges.

10. Sew the Pillar Church block to the bottom of the Stone Church block to complete the second row of the quilt. Sew the two rows together to complete the quilt center.

11. To make the borders, use the remaining two-square gold and cream units. Sew them together along their long edges to make two side borders with 21 units each. In the same manner, make the top and bottom borders with 27 units each. Sew the side borders to the quilt first. Press the seam allowances toward the appliqué blocks. Then sew the top and bottom borders to the quilt top, taking care to match intersecting seam allowances. Press.

Quilt plan

CALL TO WORSHIP

12. If you haven't already done so, prepare all the shrubbery appliqués for the various church blocks. Pin the shrubbery in place and then stitch, using the traditional appliqué stitch. The vines and leaves will be added after the quilting is complete.

Quilting and Finishing

1. Cut the backing fabric into two equal lengths, remove the selvages, and sew the pieces together to make a quilt backing that is at least 55" x 59".

2. Layer the quilt backing, batting, and quilt top and baste the layers together. Hand or machine quilt as desired. The quilt shown is machine quilted by meandering in the sky backgrounds of each church and stitching in the ditch of the checkerboard sashing and borders. I used the lines in the striped fabrics as guidelines for quilting clapboard rows in some of the churches. And as mentioned earlier, the Round Church is quilted with small brick motifs on the center of the building and larger ones on the sides.

3. Complete the appliqué work. Attach the stone pathways using the traditional appliqué stitch. Then prepare approximately 155 leaves from various shades of green. Referring to "Vines, Fences, Railings, and Casings" on page 12, prepare approximately 155" of ½"-wide finished bias vines from dark green fabric. Position the vines and leaves on the quilt, referring to the quilt photo on page 50 for placement ideas. Rearrange them until you are satisfied with the design. Appliquilt the leaves and vines, using two strands of dark green floss and an overcast stitch (see page 13).

4. Use the remaining six 2½"-wide gold solid strips to make and attach the binding, referring to page 14 as needed.

5. Label your finished quilt and enjoy it.

TATTERSALL LANE

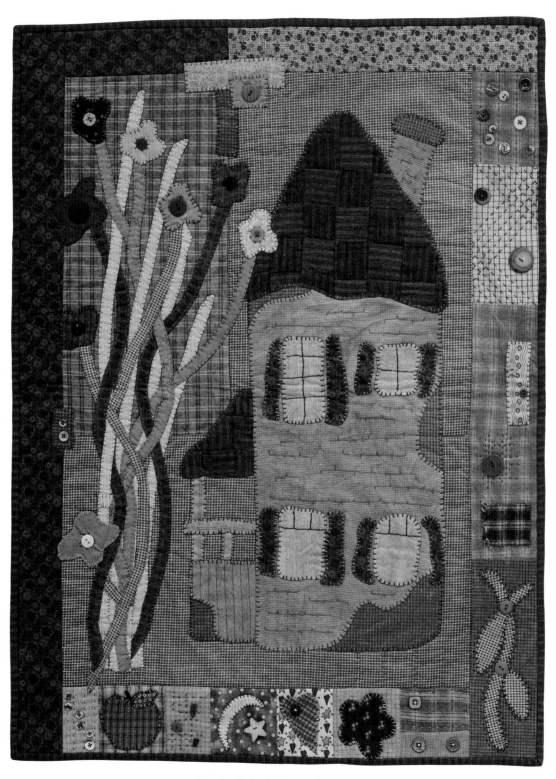

Finished Quilt Size: 24" x 32"

Tattersall Lane is an enjoyable little wall hanging to make. With just one building and less complicated patchwork than in some of the other quilts in this book, it's a project you can work up quickly for yourself or perhaps for a charming housewarming gift. I had fun creating the borders—each small square was designed in and of itself with no particular relation to anything else around it. A simple vine border would work well as an alternative if you don't share my love of "designer doodling."

Materials

Yardage is based on 42"-wide fabric.

- ⅜ yard of small blue check for background
- ⅓ yard of large blue plaid for background
- ⅓ yard of tiny tan check for house
- ⅛ yard *each* of medium and dark stripes for roofs
- ⅛ yard *each* of 4 greens for stems
- Scrap or ⅛ yard of orange or gold check for house patches
- Scrap or ⅛ yard of tan stripe for porch
- Scrap or ⅛ yard of tan plaid for porch rail
- Scraps or ⅛ yard *each* of assorted pastel solids, plaids, and prints for flowers, patches, border blocks, and motifs
- ⅛ yard of dark blue print for border
- ⅛ yard of light blue print for border
- ⅛ yard of off-white stripe for trellis
- ¼ yard of dark blue stripe for binding
- 1 yard of backing fabric
- 28" x 36" piece of batting
- Embroidery floss or pearl cotton: beige, black, gold, red, and taupe
- 40 to 45 assorted buttons
- Template plastic
- Fine-point permanent marker

Cutting

From the small blue check, cut:
1 rectangle, 11½" x 16½"
1 rectangle, 11½" x 19½"

From the large blue plaid, cut:
1 rectangle, 8½" x 16½"

From the dark blue print, cut:
1 strip, 2½" x 32½"
1 strip, 2½" x 8½"

From the light blue print, cut:
1 strip, 2½" x 14½"

From the assorted plaid scraps, cut:
1 rectangle, 3½" x 9½"
1 rectangle, 3½" x 11½"
1 rectangle, 3½" x 6½"
1 rectangle, 3½" x 4½"

From the assorted solid, plaid, and print scraps, cut:
3 squares, 3½" x 3½"
2 rectangles, 3" x 3½"
2 rectangles, 2½" x 3½"
1 rectangle, 1½" x 3½"

From the medium and dark stripes for roof, cut:
2 strips, 2" x 42", from each striped fabric; crosscut strips into 21 dark and 21 light 2" x 2" squares

From the off-white stripe, cut:
4 strips, 1" x 42"

From the assorted green fabrics, cut:
6 strips, 1" x 42"

From the dark blue stripe, cut:
3 strips, 2½" x 42"

Piecing the Quilt Top

For this small project, all the piecing is done first; then the quilt top, batting, and backing are layered and basted. The appliqué motifs are positioned and Appliquilted through all layers.

1. Sew the 8½" x 16½" blue plaid rectangle to the left of the 11½" x 16½" blue check rectangle along the 16½" edges. Press the seam allowances to one side.

2. Sew the 11½" x 19½" blue check rectangle to the bottom of the unit made in step 1. Press the seam allowances toward the bottom rectangle.

3. Use the assorted squares and rectangles to make the bottom border. Sew a 2½" x 3½" rectangle to the 1½" x 3½" rectangle. Press the seam allowances to one side. This piece will be at the right end of the lower border. Sew the remainder of the pieces together in the following order: 2½" x 3½", 3½" square, 3" x 3½", 3½" square, 3" x 3½", 3½" square, and finally the pieced square with the seam running horizontally. The completed border should measure 19½" long. Sew it to the bottom of the quilt center from step 2.

Bottom border

4. Use the assorted plaid rectangles to make the right side border. Join the rectangles along their 3½" edges in the following order: 9½", 11½", 6½", and 4½". Press all the seam

allowances in the same direction. Sew this border to the right side of the quilt with the longer rectangles at the bottom edge of the quilt.

Right border

5. Sew the 2½" x 8½" dark blue border strip to the 2½" x 14½" light blue border strip along the short edges. Press the seam allowances to one side. Sew this border to the top of the quilt so that the dark part of the border is on the left and the light part is on the right.

Top border

6. Sew the 2½" x 32½" dark blue border strip to the left edge of the quilt top. Press the seam allowances toward the border.

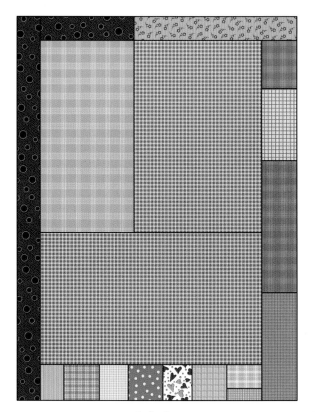
Quilt plan

Quilting and Finishing

1. Trim the backing fabric to 28" x 36" and remove the selvages.

2. Layer the quilt backing, batting, and quilt top and baste the layers together. Hand or machine quilt in the ditch of the background seams and the border seams to stabilize the quilt layers prior to adding the appliqué motifs.

3. Use the 2½"-wide dark blue stripe strips to make and attach the binding, referring to page 14 as needed.

4. Use the appliqué patterns on page 7 of the foldout sheets to prepare plastic or freezer-paper templates for all parts of the house, flowers, and border appliqués, referring to "Appliqué Templates" on page 11 as needed.

5. Trace and cut out each motif, referring to the quilt photograph on page 58 and "Materials" on page 59 for color ideas (see step 6 for cutting the roof). In the quilt shown, I used two large and six small flowers, but I suggest cutting a few more of each so that you will have a good mix to choose from when you lay out your appliqués.

6. The house and porch roofs are both cut from patchwork. Using the 2" dark- and medium-stripe squares, sew the squares into a grid, alternating the direction of the stripe as you go. For the house roof, you'll need 34 squares configured as shown at right. For the porch roof, you'll need 8 squares. Press the finished patchwork well before cutting out the roof shapes.

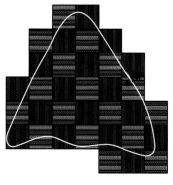

House roof   Porch roof

7. Referring to the quilt photo, position the large house piece on the quilt. Pin in place with safety pins. Then using the cutting dimensions on the foldout patterns for pieces 1, 2, and 3, cut these pieces from the orange or gold fabric and tuck them under the corners and side of the house as indicated on the pattern sheet. Pin these pieces in place with safety pins, too, for better security during the Appliquilting process.

8. For the trellis, trim the four off-white 1"-wide strips to the following lengths: 25", 24", 21", and 19". From the leftovers, cut two crossbars 2½" and 3" long. Position the trellis pieces next to the house with the longest strip farthest from the house. The short crossbar is approximately 2" from the bottom of the trellis and the 3½" crossbar is about 6" from the bottom. Place the flower stems so that they undulate along the trellis, tucking some behind the trellis bars and some over the top. Safety pin all pieces in place.

9. Continue positioning the appliqués, overlapping them as needed. Referring to "Needle-Turn Appliquilting" on page 13, stitch the pieces to the quilt in numerical order, sewing through all layers. Use coordinating or contrasting thread as desired. As you reach the top end of each trellis piece, trim the end or fold it under to taper the end to a point.

10. Add the embellishments, referring to the quilt photograph for ideas. In the quilt shown, each of the flowers has a button center. Lots of other buttons, some round and others in novelty shapes, were added to the squares and rectangles in the borders. To add to the old-time look of the quilt, I also cut a few random patches and stitched them to the borders, some with edges turned under, some with raw edges.

11. To enhance the final look of the quilt, I added bits of hand quilting. For instance, in the border square between the apple and moon, I made large quilting stitches to resemble a tic-tac-toe game, which is then sprinkled with buttons. In the right border, second rectangle from the top, I stitched a series of zigzag lines. And finally, on the house itself, I used black embroidery floss to stitch muntin bars on the windows and taupe floss to stitch lines on the house to indicate bricks.

12. Label your finished quilt and enjoy it.

ABOUT THE AUTHOR

Tonee White has been quilting for more than 15 years. She has written five books for That Patchwork Place, all of them featuring the Appliquilt technique, which she developed. *Raise the Roof* incorporates both traditional appliqué as well as her trademark Appliquilt method.

Tonee teaches and lectures nationally, and her designs can be found in quilting magazines from time to time. She also enjoys rug hooking and is presently working on coordinating quilts and rugs for the home.

Tonee lives in Scottsdale, Arizona, with her husband, Bob, and two of her seven children.

New and Bestselling Titles from

America's Best-Loved Craft & Hobby Books®
America's Best-Loved Knitting Books®

America's Best-Loved Quilt Books®

NEW RELEASES
40 Fabulous Quick-Cut Quilts
200 Knitted Blocks
Appliqué Takes Wing
Bag Boutique
Basket Bonanza
Cottage-Style Quilts
Easy Appliqué Samplers
Everyday Folk Art
Fanciful Quilts to Paper Piece
First Knits
Focus on Florals
Follow the Dots
Handknit Style
Little Box of Crocheted Hats and
    Scarves, The
Little Box of Scarves II, The
Log Cabin Quilts
Making Things
More Biblical Quilt Blocks
Painted Fabric Fun
Pleasures of Knitting, The
Quilter's Home: Spring, The
Rainbow Knits for Kids
Sarah Dallas Knitting
Scatter Garden Quilts
Shortcut to Drunkard's Path, A
Square Dance, Revised Edition
Strawberry Fair
Summertime Quilts
Tried and True

Our books are available
at bookstores and your
favorite craft, fabric,
and yarn retailers.
If you don't see
the title you're
looking for, visit us at
www.martingale-pub.com
or contact us at:
1-800-426-3126

International: 1-425-483-3313
Fax: 1-425-486-7596
Email: info@martingale-pub.com

APPLIQUÉ
Appliquilt in the Cabin
Garden Party
Stitch and Split Appliqué
Sunbonnet Sue All through the Year
Two-Block Appliqué Quilts
WOW! Wool-on-Wool Folk Art Quilts

HOLIDAY QUILTS & CRAFTS
Christmas Cats and Dogs
Christmas Delights
Hocus Pocus!
Make Room for Christmas Quilts
Welcome to the North Pole

LEARNING TO QUILT
101 Fabulous Rotary-Cut Quilts
Happy Endings, Revised Edition
Loving Stitches, Revised Edition
Magic of Quiltmaking, The
Quilter's Quick Reference Guide, The
Sensational Settings, Revised Edition
Simple Joys of Quilting, The
Your First Quilt Book (or it should be!)

PAPER PIECING
40 Bright and Bold Paper-Pieced Blocks
50 Fabulous Paper-Pieced Stars
300 Paper-Pieced Quilt Blocks
Easy Machine Paper Piecing
Hooked on Triangles
Quilter's Ark, A
Show Me How to Paper Piece

QUILTS FOR BABIES & CHILDREN
American Doll Quilts
Even More Quilts for Baby
More Quilts for Baby
Quilts for Baby
Sweet and Simple Baby Quilts

ROTARY CUTTING/SPEED PIECING
365 Quilt Blocks a Year
    Perpetual Calendar
1000 Great Quilt Blocks
Burgoyne Surrounded
Clever Quarters
Clever Quilts Encore
Endless Stars
Once More around the Block
Pairing Up
Stack a New Deck
Star-Studded Quilts
Strips and Strings
Triangle-Free Quilts

SCRAP QUILTS
More Nickel Quilts
Nickel Quilts
Scrap Frenzy
Successful Scrap Quilts

TOPICS IN QUILTMAKING
Follow-the-Line Quilting Designs
Growing Up with Quilts
Lickety-Split Quilts
More Reversible Quilts
No-Sweat Flannel Quilts
One-of-a-Kind Quilt Labels
Patchwork Showcase
Pieced to Fit
Pillow Party!
Quilter's Bounty
Quilting with My Sister
Seasonal Quilts Using Quick Bias

CRAFTS
20 Decorated Baskets
Beaded Elegance
Collage Cards
Creating with Paint
Holidays at Home
Layer by Layer
Purely Primitive
Stamp in Color
Trashformations
Vintage Workshop, The:
    Gifts for All Occasions
Warm Up to Wool
Year of Cats...in Hats!, A

KNITTING & CROCHET
365 Knitting Stitches a Year
    Perpetual Calendar
Beyond Wool
Classic Crocheted Vests
Crocheted Aran Sweaters
Crocheted Lace
Crocheted Socks!
Dazzling Knits
Garden Stroll, A
Knit it Now!
Knits from the Heart
Knitted Throws and More
Knitting with Hand-Dyed Yarns
Lavish Lace
Little Box of Scarves, The
Little Box of Sweaters, The
Pursenalities
Ultimate Knitted Tee, The